Sacred South-West Scotland

SACRED PLACES SERIES

Sacred
South-West Scotland

SCOTLAND'S CHURCHES SCHEME

SAINT ANDREW PRESS
Edinburgh

First published in 2009 by
SAINT ANDREW PRESS
121 George Street
Edinburgh
EH2 4YN

ISBN 978 0 7152 0924 0

British Library Cataloguing in Publication Data
A catalogue record for this book is available from the British Library.

Typeset in Enigma by Waverley Typesetters, Fakenham
Manufactured in Great Britain by Bell & Bain Ltd, Glasgow

BUCKINGHAM PALACE

As Patron of Scotland's Churches Scheme I warmly welcome this publication, particularly during this year of *Homecoming Scotland 2009*.

The story of the heritage and culture of Scotland would be lacking significantly without a strong focus on its churches and sacred sites. I am sure that this guidebook will be a source of information and enjoyment both to the people of Scotland and to our visitors during this memorable year.

Anne

Scotland's Churches Scheme

Scotland's Churches Scheme is an ecumenical charitable trust, providing an opportunity to access the nation's living heritage of faith by assisting 'living' churches to:

- Promote spiritual understanding by enabling the public to appreciate all buildings designed for worship and active as living churches
- Work together with others to make the Church the focus of the community
- Open their doors with a welcoming presence
- Tell the story of the building (however old or new), its purpose and heritage (artistic, architectural and historical)
- Provide information for visitors, young and old

The Scheme has grown rapidly since its inception in 1994 and there are now more than 1200 churches in membership. These churches are spread across Scotland and across the denominations.

The *Sacred Scotland* theme promoted by Scotland's Churches Scheme focuses on the wish of both visitors and local communities to be able to access our wonderful range of church buildings in a meaningful way, whether the visit be occasioned by spiritual or heritage motivation or both. The Scheme can advise and assist member churches on visitor welcome, and with its range of 'how-to' brochures, provide information on research, presentation, security and other live issues. The Scheme, with its network of local representatives, encourages the opening of doors, the care of tourists and locals alike, and offers specific services such as the provision of grants for organ playing.

Sacred Scotland (www.sacredscotland.org.uk), the web-site of Scotland's Churches Scheme, opens the door to Scotland's story by exploring living traditions of faith in city, town, village and island across the country. The site is a portal to access information on Scotland's churches of all denominations and a starting point for your special journeys.

We are delighted to be working with Saint Andrew Press in the publication of this series of regional guides to Scotland's churches. This volume, *South-West Scotland*, is one of three being published in 2009 (the others are *Edinburgh and Midlothian* and *Fife and the Forth Valley*) to be followed by a further three books in 2010 and again in 2011 when the whole country will have been covered. We are grateful to the authors of the introductory articles, Professor John Hume, one of our Trustees, and Donna Brewster for their expert contributions to our understanding of sacred places.

The growth of 'spiritual tourism' worldwide is reflected in the million-plus people who visit Scotland's religious sites annually. We hope that the information in this book will be useful in bringing alive the heritage as well as the ministry of welcome which our churches offer. In the words of our President, Lady Marion Fraser: 'we all owe a deep debt of gratitude to the many people of vision who work hard and imaginatively to create a lasting and peaceful atmosphere which you will carry away with you as a special memory when you leave'.

DR BRIAN FRASER
Director

Invitation to Pilgrimage
South-west Scotland

Beauty and Character

Thomas Carlyle is reputed to have advised Queen Victoria that the most beautiful road in all her kingdoms was the Galloway road between Gatehouse of Fleet and Ferrytown of Cree. Carlyle's famed acquaintance John Ruskin, describing the southern part of Scotland, wrote in the same period:

> This space of low mountain ground, with the eternal sublimity of its rocky seashores, of its stormy seas and dangerous sands; its strange and mighty crags ... and its pathless moorlands, haunted by the driving cloud, had been of more import in the true world's history than all the lovely countries of the South, except only Palestine. (*Praeterita*, Vol. III)

More than a century after those words were written, in a part of Scotland still quite unspoiled by any great urbanisation, sites that mark mankind's spiritual quests throughout all the ages can still be found in abundance in all areas of the sacred south-west of Scotland.

Early Civilisation

Many prehistoric stones, cairns, and circles dot the hauntingly beautiful landscape, each ancient site evoking an awareness that the earliest settlers of prehistory were concerned to establish a relationship with the unseen spiritual world and acknowledge their sense of a life beyond death.

Scotland's Cradle of Christianity

The earliest Christian stone in Scotland, the Latinus Stone, is on display at Whithorn. A fifth-century Christian testimony, carved tellingly on this stone, was discovered within the precincts of the medieval priory in the area always believed to be the Candida Casa site established by St Ninian in that same fifth century. From shorelines near Whithorn, to the east across the Solway can be seen the Lake District Hills; to the south, the Isle of Man; and, to the west over the Irish Sea, the Mountains of Mourne in Ireland. The Galloway Hills, framing the scene to the north, form the boundary between Galloway and neighbouring Ayrshire. According to the Venerable Bede, in this peninsular corner barely within the grasp of the Roman Empire, the Romano-British prince Bishop Ninian founded a place of learning and a centre for evangelistic outreach into the places described in his time as the 'ends of the earth'.

The name of Ninian, earliest and once foremost of all Scottish saints, marks ancient Christian sites from the north of England, through the central belt of Scotland, on up the eastern coast of the country to the very islands of Orkney and Shetland. Among those influenced by the work begun at Whithorn were many of the great leaders of the Celtic Christianity movement of succeeding generations.

Medieval Monuments

Dating from later centuries, medieval church, priory and monastic sites, many now lying mostly ruinous and often neglected, are associated with a number of the most famous personages and events of Scottish history. Cruggleton Castle hosted King David of Scotland in conference with Fergus of Galloway, both encountered by St Malachy who took time to heal a deaf mute along the way while pleading for the establishment of Cistercian monasteries in the area. The horror of sanctuary defiled by political murder was witnessed by the walls of Greyfriars Kirk in Dumfries. The glowing red sandstone of Sweetheart Abbey yet pays tribute to the love of a widowed Devorgilla for her husband John Balliol. Every Scottish monarch for a thousand years came to Whithorn. Robert the Bruce, James IV and Mary Queen of Scots made dramatic pilgrimages there. Crossraguel Abbey at Maybole was the scene of the debate between the Reformer John Knox and Abbot Quentin Kennedy, an encounter credited with changing the course of the history of a nation's faith.

Covenanter Memories

After the Reformation, the south-west of Scotland became the setting for many of the most stirring and tragic events of the national religious storm that rolled on for over fifty years, the period of the seventeenth century's Covenanter struggles. The saintly Guthries, Samuel Rutherford of Anwoth, Alexander Peden, the Prophet of the Covenant, John Welsh of Irongray, the Cameron brothers who gave their name to a movement that lived on for centuries, the two Margarets, one elderly and one a girl, both said to have drowned in the tidal waters of the Bladnoch River at Wigtown, and the young, golden preacher James Renwick of Moniaive, one of the last to be put to death for the cause, were all people of the south-west. The places where they lived their lives and made their courageous witness, as well as their graves, are sought out by many who come from all over the world to find them, modern people who attribute their present spiritual freedoms and sense of toleration to those whose courage and convictions were displayed in life, and in death, during less tolerant times.

Faith in a Modern Age

During the last three centuries, the ancient parish churches have been rebuilt. Other Christian denominations have established places of worship in many towns and villages of the south-west of Scotland as well, meeting in dedicated buildings, public halls, or homes; becoming, themselves, part of the pattern of providing places of fellowship, instruction and witness that continues the work begun by Ninian, 1,600 years ago. People of other faiths, too, find a home and acceptance, a sanctuary, in this quiet and beautiful area of Scotland.

Modern pilgrim visitors are delighted by the rich evidence of history and the sense of a continuing, living faith in the area when they come to the south-west of Scotland. Whether they seek out the most ancient stones of mysterious meaning at Cairn Holy, look for the beautifully carved graffiti crosses in Ninian's cave down leafy Physgill Glen, trace the Celtic knotwork patterns in thousand-year-old stone crosses, wander in the red sandstone cloisters that speak of Devorgilla's love, sing with friends in the bell-like chapterhouse of the ruins of Glenluce Abbey, hear echoes of the voice of John Knox in the Maybole ruins, read the tender letters of Samuel Rutherford while sitting within the walls of his beloved Kirk of Anwoth, lay their tribute at the grave of Prophet Peden, seek out Covenanter memories on a bleak Fenwick moor, stand on the tidal grasses by the martyrs' stake at Wigtown, or gaze at beautiful Victorian windows in south-west churches while they worship with modern inhabitants, they become part of the movement that has gone on through centuries, a need to search out, and often to find what they seek, in a place of great natural beauty.

Some arrive as members of large church groups; others come in smaller, tutored bands; many come as individuals, on a personal pilgrimage. They may find themselves at the Isle of Whithorn, a harbour village that for centuries has embraced the arrival of pilgrims from all over the world. There they find the Witness Cairn where they are invited to lay a stone marking their own, unique, spiritual quest.

DONNA BREWSTER
Whithorn Trust

Introduction

Sacred South-west Scotland

South-west Scotland is in the context of this booklet an omnibus term to describe the old counties of Ayrshire (now East, North and South Ayrshire), Wigtownshire, Kirkcudbrightshire and Dumfriesshire (now Dumfries and Galloway). These are parts of Scotland not as well-known as they should be, rich in historical associations and monuments, with areas of remarkable natural beauty. The northern parts of Ayrshire are thoroughly lowland in character, but a large part of South Ayrshire and much of Dumfries and Galloway are in the Southern Uplands which separate the latter from the central lowlands of Scotland. This difference in the landforms reflects a different underlying geology. Much of Ayrshire was rich in coal and ironstone, which led to its industrialisation from the late eighteenth century onwards. Apart from local deposits of lead ore, of coal in north and east Dumfriesshire, and of building stone, Dumfries and Galloway had little in the way of economic mineral resources. Industrialisation was patchy, and did not result in the development of large urban settlements in that area. Pastoral farming, with some arable cultivation, was and is the main land use both in Galloway and in rural Ayrshire. It was out of this farming background that Robert Burns came. The pattern of dispersed rural population arising from this style of farming is reflected in the pattern of church building, and indeed of denominational allegiance, of the rural parts of the south-west.

There are few large towns in the south-west. Dumfries, Ayr, Irvine and Kilmarnock are the largest,

Fig. 1. Dundrennan Abbey

Fig. 2. Kilwinning Abbey

and have church buildings reflecting their local metropolitan status. The Ayrshire coast became, after the development of railways, popular with well-to-do people from Glasgow and inland Ayrshire as places to live (and to play golf), and also attractive to holidaymakers. Largs, Saltcoats, Troon, Prestwick, Ayr and Girvan all developed as resorts, and the churches in these places reflected their dual (or multiple) functions.

This brief socio-economic background is helpful in looking at the history of the churches in the area. Before Christianity, however, there were sites which one can interpret as having been of religious significance. Among these are the stone circle at Torhouse, near Wigtown, settings of standing stones at Laggangairn and Drumtroddan, with nearby cup and ring marks. There are also burial cairns, which were probably places of veneration. Of these Cairn Holy I, near Creetown, with its 'courtyard', is the most striking. The first Christian mission to Scotland appears to have been that of St Ninian, who brought Roman Catholicism to Whithorn in the late fourth century. Subsequently, his influence was complemented by Viking and Northumbrian settlement in Dumfries and Galloway, of which the Northumbrian Ruthwell Cross (c.680) in the parish church there, is evidence. After the unification of Scotland in the eleventh century, successive monarchs, notably David I, created a structure of religious administration which also to a degree was a civil administration. This included the division of the country into parishes, and the establishment of monasteries. In south-west Scotland the monasteries were established by noble families, rather than by the monarch. There were six in all, Sweetheart (1273), Dundrennan (1142, Fig. 1), Tongland (c.1218), Glenluce (1192), Crossraguel (1214) and

Fig. 3. Maybole Collegiate Church

Fig. 4. Monkton Old Parish Church

Kilwinning (late twelfth century, Fig. 2). The founding of a monastery was expensive, and later nobles founded collegiate churches. The remains of two of these survive, at Lincluden, near Dumfries (1389), and at Maybole (c.1382, Fig. 3). Few of the pre-Reformation parish churches survive. Probably the most remarkable is Symington, in South Ayrshire (**106**), a twelfth-century Norman church (restored in 1919), much of whose original fabric survives, and which is still in use for worship. There are ruins of a number of others, most of which remained in use, with alterations after the Reformation, until replacement churches were built in the eighteenth or nineteenth centuries. These include St Nicholas Old and Monkton Old (both thirteenth century, Fig. 4), Buittle Old (thirteenth–sixteenth century), and 'Alloway's Auld Haunted Kirk' (Fig. 5). Many of the parish church sites in the area appear to be ancient worship sites, and some of the buildings currently in use may well incorporate pre-Reformation masonry. The Auld Kirk, Kilbirnie (**24**, 1430 on) and Straiton (**105**, south transept c.1510) certainly do.

The Reformation resulted in the closure of the monasteries and collegiate churches, though the monks were allowed to stay on until they died. The pattern of parishes remained, however, and became a key element in the Reformed Church. Every parish was to have a school, and a parish church. As a measure of hygiene, the practice of burying bodies inside churches was ended, and landed families accordingly started to construct burial 'aisles' adjoining churches. Several of these still exist, as at Largs (1636, Fig. 6), Kilmaurs (**68**, 1600),

Fig. 5. Alloway Old Kirk

Fig. 6. The Skelmorlie Aisle, Largs Old Parish Church

Ballantrae (c.1601, Fig. 7) and Old Dailly (seventeenth century). The largest is the 'Queir' at Terregles (1585), and the most elaborate the Queensberry burial aisle at Durisdeer (**166**, 1697–1708). In other cases, free-standing mausolea were built in churchyards, or the roofless ruins of churches were used as burial areas. There are good examples of early mausolea in Largs old churchyard and at Dunlop (**54**). An early post-Reformation church, at least in part, is St Quivox, Auchincruive (**85**, 1595 on).

The system of dioceses, for oversight of parishes, which had been a feature of the pre-Reformation church, was revived by James VI in 1611, but does not seem to have met with any significant opposition. It was quite otherwise with Charles I's attempt to align the Church of Scotland with the Church of England. This was an important cause of the revolt against the monarch which resulted in his execution, and the establishment of Oliver Cromwell as the 'Lord Protector' of the United Kingdom. In Scotland, opposition to Charles's intentions crystallised in the signing of the National Covenant in 1638. The Solemn League and Covenant, signed in 1643, brought together a more radical group of opponents to the involvement of the civil authority with the church. It received significant support in the south-west, and when, after Charles II was restored to the throne of the United Kingdom in 1660, he restored episcopacy, the 'Covenanters' remained opposed to the new system.

Resistance to the established church was opposed by armed force in a manner which is still resented in the south-west. Ayr has one of the few churches built by Government during Cromwell's rule. This (the Auld Kirk, **78**) was constructed in 1654 to replace a medieval church, the site of which was required to build an artillery fort to protect the town. The much altered tower

Fig. 7. The Kennedy Aisle, Ballantrae

of the earlier building survives (Fig. 8). Another building of great interest from this period is the roofless old church of New Cumnock (1657), which is on the one hand a very early example of a T-plan church built as such, and on the other a late example of Gothic detailing.

After the death of Charles I, his brother, James, succeeded to the throne. James was a devout Roman Catholic, and showed every intention of making that the state religion of the United Kingdom. It was fear of that possibility that led to the removal of James from the throne

Fig. 8. St John's Tower, Ayr

and his replacement by William of Orange and his wife Mary, as joint monarchs. William brought with him William Carstares, who had been exiled from Scotland for his opposition to Charles I's religious policy. Carstares brought to William's policy a Dutch Reformed perspective, and the restoration of presbyterian church government to the Church of Scotland which William implemented owed much to Carstares's thinking. This restoration was resented by two groups in Scottish society, both fairly prominent in the south-west. On the one hand, some Covenanters felt that the new structure was still too close to the state, and on the other some people who had become attached to the Episcopalian system resented its demise. Though both groups were outlawed (the latter on suspicion of Jacobitism), they remained active 'underground' until they were allowed to come into the open in the later eighteenth century. The successors to the Covenanters eventually became an organised church – the Reformed Presbyterians.

Fig. 9. Reformed Presbyterian Church, Stranraer

Fig. 10. Ayr Free Church (ex Reformed Presbyterian)

Their last congregation in the area was in Stranraer (church built 1824, Fig. 9), but Ayr Free Church meets in a former Reformed Presbyterian building (1832, Fig. 10) and there is another, much altered, one at Quarrelwood, Dumfriesshire. The Episcopalians have been much more successful as a denomination.

Several churches in the south-west date from the seventeenth century, in whole or in part. Of particular interest are Fenwick (**55**, 1643) and St Columba's Stewarton (**75**, 1696), both on a Greek cross plan. These are (with the Auld Kirk of Ayr) examples of a church layout with apparent links with the worship patterns of the Danish Lutheran church. Kirkmaiden (**121**, 1638), Sorn (**73**, 1658, but much altered) and Auchinleck Old (1683, now a mortuary chapel, Fig. 11) are examples of the simple, almost domestic churches characteristic of Scotland from the mid-seventeenth to the mid-

Fig. 11. Auchinleck Old Parish Church

eighteenth century. There are ruins of a number of others, such as Anwoth Old (1626, Fig. 12), Girthon Old, and Monigaff, which may incorporate medieval fabric. The fifteenth-century Auld Kirk at Kilbirnie (**24**) was twice extended, in 1592 and in 1642. In about 1705 the ornate wooden Crawford Loft was installed, the most remarkable church furnishing of its period in Scotland.

In the mid to late eighteenth century, road improvement opened up new markets for agricultural produce, and new

Fig. 12. Anwoth Old Parish Church

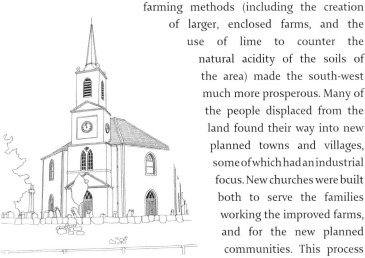

Fig. 13. Dreghorn Parish Church

farming methods (including the creation of larger, enclosed farms, and the use of lime to counter the natural acidity of the soils of the area) made the south-west much more prosperous. Many of the people displaced from the land found their way into new planned towns and villages, some of which had an industrial focus. New churches were built both to serve the families working the improved farms, and for the new planned communities. This process gained momentum in the early nineteenth century, and was particularly effective in Dumfries and Galloway. Another important trend was the growth of the trading burghs, on the basis both of overseas and local trade. Local pride was often expressed by the building of churches with 'classical' steeples, particularly common in Ayrshire. The finest early examples are Irvine Old Kirk (**20**, 1774) and Dreghorn (1780, Fig. 13). The only Dumfries and Galloway example is Annan Old (**151**, 1789, steeple 1801). Other interesting later eighteenth-century churches include the architecturally refined Kirkoswald (**97**, 1777) and Catrine (**45**, 1792), and the unusually large Holywood (1779). Kirkmichael, Ayrshire (**96**, 1787), Ochiltree (1789, Fig. 14) and Kirkgunzeon (1790) are good examples of the smaller, simpler churches of the period.

One aspect of the reform of the Church of Scotland in 1690 was a requirement on the part of the major landowners (heritors) in a parish (and the Town Council in a burgh) to provide church buildings on a scale appropriate to the population, and to maintain them. With this,

Fig. 14. Ochiltree Parish Church

Fig. 15. The former Irvine Relief Church

came the right to appoint ministers (patronage), even if congregations disapproved. The resentment this caused resulted in two major 'secessions' from the Church of Scotland in the eighteenth century. The history of these is too complex to discuss here, where it will suffice to say that the earlier took place in 1733, and the later in 1761, to form the Relief Church. They later united, in 1847 (see below). There are few surviving buildings constructed by these bodies. One is still in use for worship: Irvine Relief (1773, Fig. 15), now an evangelical church. There are former Secession churches in Beith (Head Street, 1782) and Tarbolton, and former Relief churches in Ayr (Cathcart Street, 1816), Stranraer (1821, Fig. 16), and at Burnhead, near Penpont (1839).

Patronage continued until 1874, and remained an issue until then. After 1810 the heritors, faced with rising population in both town and country, often chose to replace older buildings with a pattern of church recently described as 'Heritors' Gothic' characterised by pointed windows and square towers, often with pinnacles. These are very common throughout the area, though they vary widely in layout and detailing. Many of the earlier ones were built in Dumfries and Galloway, as focal points in rural areas, such as Buittle (1819), Kells (**146**, 1822), Kirkmahoe (1822), Stoneykirk (1827) and Glencairn (**168**, 1836). Ayrshire examples include Mauchline (**69**, 1829), New Cumnock (**71**, 1833) and Coylton (1836, Fig. 17). The towers were built to house bells, and sometimes clocks. In the late 1830s the first Gothic Revival churches with steeples were built in the area. These were among the earliest in Scotland. The very first were Kirkcudbright (**141**, 1838) and Penninghame, Newton Stewart (**124**, 1840). The type became very common later in the nineteenth century.

With increasing population and wealth came religious diversity. From the 1730s, those members of the Church of Scotland who resented the

Fig. 16. The former Stranraer Relief Church

Fig. 17. Coylton Parish Church

power of the State and of the heritors in the running of the church (and especially the right of the heritors to appoint ministers) had, as described above, broken away in a series of 'secessions'. These movements, though they did not originate in the south-west, became popular there (see above). There were also revivals of the Scottish Episcopal Church, and of the Roman Catholic Church. An early Scottish Episcopal church was built in Dumfries (1817, now a public house) and St Peter's, Dalbeattie (**138**, 1814) is a pioneering Roman Catholic building. The latter Church expanded markedly after the 1840s with large-scale immigration from Ireland, initially in response to famine, but later to satisfy growing demands for industrial labour in Ayrshire (see below).

Before that, however, three other important moves in Church organisation had taken place. The first was a coming-together in 1820 of what had become the fragmented secessions, descendants of the original secession of 1733, to form the United Secession Church. There are surviving United Secession churches at Kilwinning (now Free, 1824), Stewarton (John Knox, 1828, Fig. 18), Cumnock (now a surgery, 1831), Annan (Erskine, 1834–5, disused) and Kilwinning (Erskine, 1838, **27**, now independent). In 1847 the United Secession Church joined the Relief Church (formed in 1761) to create the United Presbyterian Church, which proved a formidable denomination for the rest of the nineteenth century. The third, and most cataclysmic development, was the Disruption in the Church of Scotland, when about a third of the ministers of the established Church of Scotland left that church to found the Free

Fig. 18. John Knox Church, Stewarton

Church of Scotland. As in the eighteenth-century secessions, the main issue was patronage. The Free Church, though very influential, proved to be less dominant in south-west Scotland than in other parts of the country.

The new Free Church had immediately to build churches and manses on a large scale. Some of the first generation of Free churches, built in the 1840s, still survive, such as Girthon and Anwoth Free, Gatehouse (1844, now in other use), Isle of Whithorn (**118**, 1843–4) and Lewis Street Gospel Hall, Stranraer, built as a Free church between 1843 and 1846, but many were subsequently replaced or rebuilt. Competitive church building between the 'big three' Presbyterian denominations (Church of Scotland, United Presbyterian and Free) was a feature of the later nineteenth century, especially in the towns and large villages. Many of the buildings were large steepled Gothic Revival structures. Probably the first was Irvine Trinity (Free, 1863, Fig. 19), a striking example of the original work of F. T. W. Pilkington. The others are more conventional, and include Free churches in Lockerbie (1866), Darvel (1885, Fig. 20), Ayr (1893); and Cumnock (1899, Fig. 21), United Presbyterian churches in Troon (St Meddan's, **110**, 1888–9), Largs (Clark Memorial, **31**, 1892) and Moffat (1890–2, now flats); and Church of

Fig. 19. The former Irvine Trinity Church

Fig. 20. The former Irvinebank and Easton Memorial Church (ex Darvel Free)

Fig. 21. Crichton Memorial Church, Cumnock (ex Free)

Scotland churches at Dalbeattie (1878–80), Girvan (1883), Ayr (St Leonard's, **83**, 1886) and Largs (St Columba's, **32**, 1892). Others had towers such as the odd Rerrick, Dundrennan (1864–6), Castle Douglas Parish (now a theatre, 1869, tower 1890), St James's, Ayr (**82**, 1885), Lamlash (**7**, 1886) and the extraordinary Crichton Memorial hospital church at Dumfries (**160**, 1896–7). The Scottish Episcopal and Roman Catholic churches also expanded in the area. Large Episcopal churches were built in Millport (the Cathedral of the Isles, **15**, 1849–51), Kilmarnock (Holy Trinity, **62**, 1857, 1876), Dumfries (St John the Evangelist, **163**, 1867–8), Challoch (All Saints, **113**, 1872) and Ayr (Holy Trinity, **79**, 1888), as well as many smaller ones. Most of the early Roman Catholic churches were fairly small, but St Joseph's, Kilmarnock (1847, Fig. 22) was an exception. Construction of larger buildings began in the 1880s, with St John the Evangelist, Cumnock (**48**, 1882) and the remarkable Byzantine St Sophia's, Galston (**57**, 1886). The outstanding

Fig. 22. St Joseph's Roman Catholic Church, Kilmarnock

Roman Catholic church of the period before the First World war is Our Lady and St Meddan's, Troon (**108**, 1910), which can stand comparison with the best churches of the period anywhere in Scotland.

The impetus for church building by the Church of Scotland was increased from the 1880s by the 'Scoto-Catholic' movement, which aimed to

Fig. 23. Southwick Church

Fig. 24. St Nicholas's Parish Church, Prestwick

reintroduce some aspects of medieval worship. The styles favoured by this movement were scholarly revivals of late Scots Gothic and Romanesque. The outstanding example of the former is St Molios, Shiskine, on Arran (**10**, 1889). There are fine small Romanesque Revival churches at Southwick (1891, Fig. 23) and Dalton (**158**, 1895), and important larger ones at Saltcoats (**36**, St Cuthbert's, 1908), Prestwick (St Nicholas, 1908, Fig. 24) and Colvend (**135**, 1911). The Free and United Presbyterian churches came together in 1900 as the United Free Church, which continued to build new churches until the First World War. The finest are probably Henderson, Kilmarnock (**63**, 1907), the Arthur Memorial, New Cumnock (1912, no longer a church, Fig. 25) and Portland, Troon (**109**, 1914).

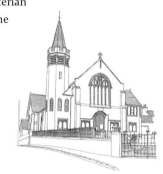

Fig. 25. The former Arthur Memorial Church, New Cumnock (ex United Free)

The First World War brought an end to church building in the area, except for a remarkable group of churches in Dumfriesshire, whose construction was prompted by the establishment of a gigantic complex of explosives factories to meet the needs of the war. The villages of Eastriggs and Gretna were expanded to house workers, and new churches built for them, in 1917–18. Scottish Episcopal and Roman Catholic churches were constructed in both communities, and also a Church of Scotland (St Andrew's). The best architecturally are the Episcopal churches in Eastriggs (**167**) and Gretna (**169**), and the Byzantine Roman Catholic church in Gretna (Fig. 26), now alas disused.

Fig. 26. The former St Ninian's Roman Catholic Church, Gretna

Fig. 27. Shortlees Parish Church, Kilmarnock

After the First World War, adverse economic circumstances dramatically reduced the rate of church building. A new Scottish Episcopal church (St Ninian's) was built in Prestwick in 1926, and a new Church of Scotland church at Middlebie in 1929. In 1929 the United Free and the Church of Scotland amalgamated, as the Church of Scotland. The new church over a period rationalised its building stock, usually closing the United Free churches,

many of which found new uses. This experience is different from that in the Highlands, where the former Church of Scotland buildings were usually chosen for closure. New Roman Catholic churches were built in the 1930s, at Prestwick (St Quivox, **104**, 1933), Kilwinning (St Winin's, **29**, 1937) and Ardrossan (St Peter in Chains, **2**, 1938). The last-named is one of the finest interwar churches anywhere in Scotland.

Fig. 28. Castlehill Parish Church, Ayr

Church building on any scale was not resumed until after the Second World War, when major programmes of public housing were undertaken around many of the towns in the area, especially in Ayrshire. These were partly to house returning servicemen, partly to allow slum clearance, and partly to cope with the expansion of coalmining and of other new industries. Much of this housing was in new, more-or-less self-contained estates, and part of the process involved building new churches

Fig. 29. Lochside Parish Church, Dumfries

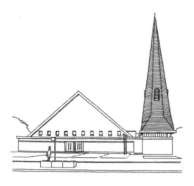

Fig. 30. St Teresa's Roman Catholic Church, Dumfries

and other community facilities. Many of the Church of Scotland churches were constructed as a result of a 'Church Extension' programme, with buildings designed in the first instance as 'hall churches' for multi-purpose use. These included Shortlees, Kilmarnock (1951, Fig. 27) Dalmilling, Ayr (1953), Lincluden, Dumfries (1953) and St Ninian's, Netherthird, Cumnock (1955). Some, such as St John's, Onthank, St Ninian's, Bellfield, Kilmarnock, Castlehill, Ayr (Fig. 28), and Lochside, Dumfries (1964-5, Fig. 29) later had single-purpose worship spaces added. Other notable Church of Scotland churches of the postwar period are St Andrew's, Irvine (21, 1957) and the little church of Sandhead (126), south of Stranraer. The Roman Catholic churches of the

Fig. 31. St John Ogilvie's Roman Catholic Church, Irvine

period included the Cathedral of the Good Shepherd, Ayr (1955), St Teresa's (1956-8, Fig. 30) and St Andrew's (1963-4), Dumfries, and St Paul's, Ayr (84, 1967). All of these were architecturally innovative, the finest probably St Teresa's. The creation of Irvine New Town also provided an opportunity for the building of new churches, including St Peter's, Bourtreehill (1976) and Girdle Toll (23, 1990) for the Church of Scotland, and St John Ogilvie, Bourtreehill

Fig. 32. Ardrossan Congregational Church

Fig. 33. Maybole Baptist Church

(1982, Fig. 31), for the Roman Catholics. The first new Church of Scotland church of the twenty-first century was the circular Mansefield Trinity, Kilwinning (**30**, 2001), a 'translation' from an old town-centre building.

So far, this narrative has been principally about the major denominations, but mention should be made of a number of the less well-represented ones. Congregationalism has been notable in the area, and is still strong in Ayrshire, especially in Ardrossan (1905, Fig. 32), Cumnock (**49**, 1883) and Kilmarnock (**67**, 1860). There are a number of Baptist (Fig. 33) and Methodist congregations, as well as congregations of the Free and United Free churches who stayed out of the twentieth-century unions. There are several Gospel halls of various branches of the Christian Brethren, the halls of the Salvation Army, as well as buildings used by the Church of the Nazarene (Fig. 34) and other 'holiness' churches, and by the Church of Christ Jesus of the Latter-day Saints (Mormons). Declining church membership has also resulted in the use for worship by some congregations of schools and other community buildings. A particularly interesting development has been

Fig. 34. Church of the Nazarene, Ardrossan

the construction of a new 'church centre' in the village of Monkton (**100**, 2004), with much emphasis of its use for community purposes during the week. It is certainly true that the Church is alive and well in south-west Scotland, a tribute to the eternal truths it embodies, and to St Ninian and other missionaries who brought Christianity to the area.

Professor John R. Hume
Universities of Glasgow and St Andrews

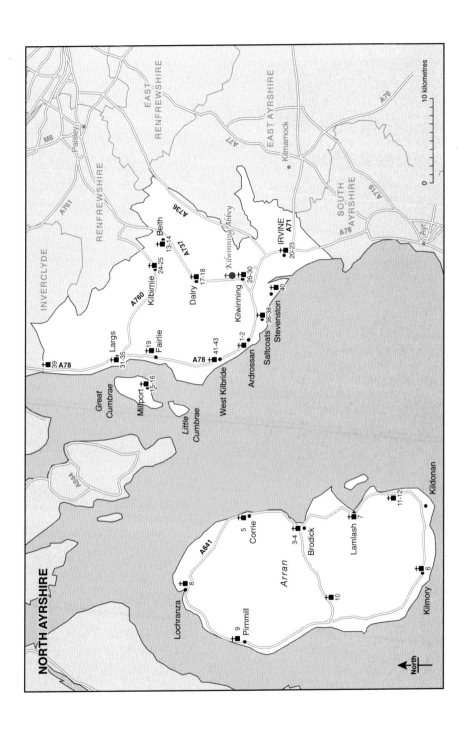

NORTH AYRSHIRE

INVERCLYDE

RENFREWSHIRE

A761

M8

Paisley

A737

EAST
RENFREWSHIRE

A77

EAST AYRSHIRE

Kilmarnock

A76

10 kilometres

0

SOUTH
AYRSHIRE

A78

A79

to Ayr

A736

Kilwinning Abbey

Beith
13-14

A737

Kilbirnie
24-25

Dalry
17-18

Kilwinning
26-30

IRVINE
A71
20-23

A760

Stevenston
40

Saltcoats
36-38

Largs

Fairlie
19

A78
41-43

Ardrossan
1-2

West Kilbride

A78

39 A78

31-35

Great
Cumbrae

Millport
15-16

Little
Cumbrae

A841

Lochranza
8

Pirnmill
9

Corrie
5

Arran

Brodick
3-4

Lamlash
7

10

11-12

Kilmory
6

Kildonan

North

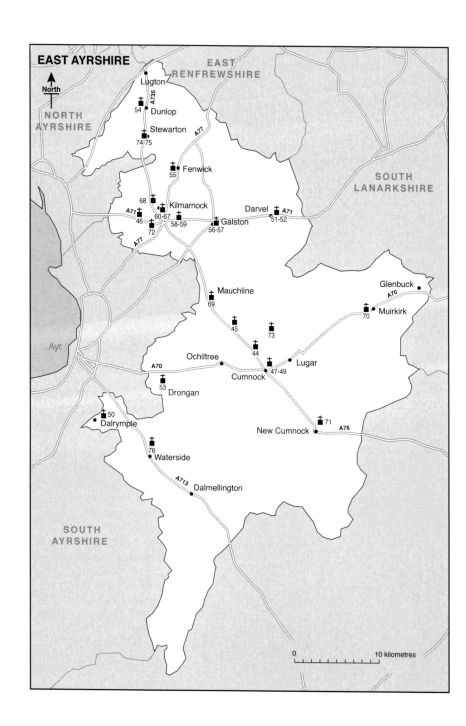

EAST AYRSHIRE

North

EAST
RENFREWSHIRE

NORTH
AYRSHIRE

SOUTH
LANARKSHIRE

Lugton

54 Dunlop
A735

Stewarton
74-75

A77

Fenwick
55

68
Kilmarnock
A71
46
60-67
72
58-59

Darvel
51-52
A71

Galston
56-57

Mauchline
69

Glenbuck

A70
Muirkirk
70

45

73

44

Ochiltree

A70

Lugar
47-49

Cumnock

53
Drongan

50
Dalrymple

New Cumnock
71
A76

76
Waterside

A713
Dalmellington

SOUTH
AYRSHIRE

Ayr

A77

A71

0   10 kilometres

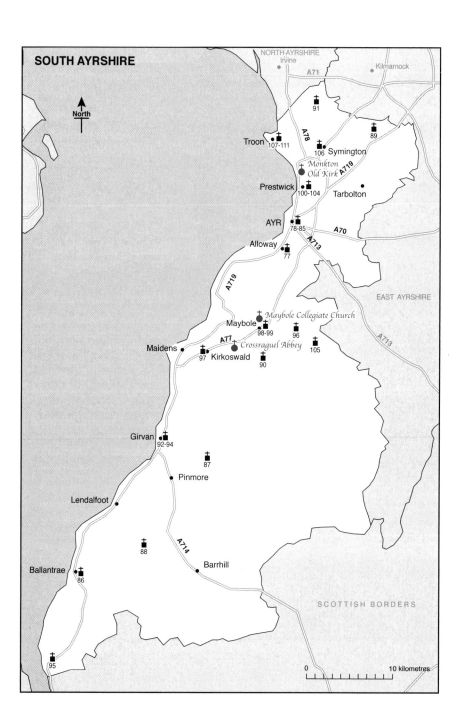

SOUTH AYRSHIRE

North

NORTH AYRSHIRE
Irvine
A71
Kilmarnock

91

Troon
107-111   106   A78   89
Symington

A719
Monkton
Old Kirk
Prestwick
100-104   Tarbolton

AYR
78-85   A70
A713
Alloway
77

A719
EAST AYRSHIRE
A713

Maybole Collegiate Church
Maybole
98-99   96
A77   Crossraguel Abbey   105
Maidens
97   Kirkoswald
90

Girvan
92-94

87
Pinmore

Lendalfoot

88   A714
Barrhill

Ballantrae
86

SCOTTISH BORDERS

95

0   10 kilometres

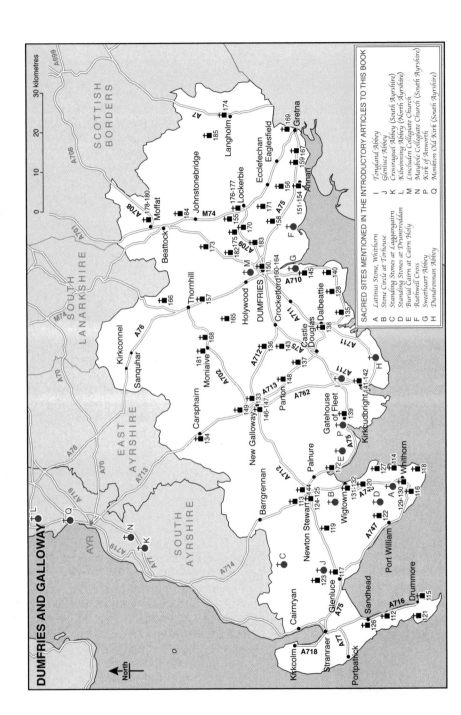

DUMFRIES AND GALLOWAY

North

0	10	20	30 kilometres	

SCOTTISH BORDERS

SOUTH LANARKSHIRE

EAST AYRSHIRE

SOUTH AYRSHIRE

SACRED SITES MENTIONED IN THE INTRODUCTORY ARTICLES TO THIS BOOK

A Latinus Stone, Whithorn
B Stone Circle at Torhouse
C Standing Stones at Laggangairn
D Standing Stones at Drumtroddan
E Burial Cairn at Cairn Holy
F Ruthwell Cross
G Sweetheart Abbey
H Dundrennan Abbey

I Tongland Abbey
J Glenluce Abbey
K Crossraguel Abbey (South Ayrshire)
L Kilwinning Abbey (North Ayrshire)
M Lincluden Collegiate Church
N Maybole Collegiate Church (South Ayrshire)
O Kirk of Anworth
P Monkton Old Kirk (South Ayrshire)

Gretna
Annan
Eaglesfield
Ecclefechan
Langholm
Lockerbie
Johnstonebridge
Moffat
Beattock
Thornhill
Kirkconnel
Sanquhar
Carsphairn
Moniaive
Holywood
DUMFRIES
Crocketford
Castle Douglas
Dalbeattie
Parton
New Galloway
Gatehouse of Fleet
Kirkcudbright
Palnure
Barrgrennan
Newton Stewart
Wigtown
Whithorn
Port William
Drummore
Sandhead
Glenluce
Stranraer
Cairnryan
Portpatrick
Kirkcolm
AYR

How to use this Guide

Entries are arranged by local authority area, with large areas sub-divided for convenience. The number preceding each entry refers to the map. Each entry is followed by symbols for access and facilities:

Å Ordnance Survey reference	🔊 Hearing induction loop for the deaf
🏠 Denomination	🧑 Welcomers and guides on duty
⊕ Church website	📖 Guidebooks and souvenirs available/for sale
• Regular services	
○ Church events	❀ Church Recorders' Inventory NADFAS (NADFAS)
• Opening arrangements	👤 Features for children/link with schools
♿ Wheelchair access for partially abled	
wc Toilets available for visitors	🍴 Refreshments
	Ⓐ Category A listing
wc Toilets adapted for the disabled available for visitors	Ⓑ Category B listing
	Ⓒ Category C listing

Category A: Buildings of national or international importance, either architectural or historic, or fine little-altered examples of some particular period, style or building type.

Category B: Buildings of regional or more than local importance, or major examples of some particular period, style or building type which may have been altered.

Category C: Buildings of local importance, lesser examples of any period, style, or building type, as originally constructed or moderately altered; and simple traditional buildings which group well with others in categories A and B.

The information appearing in the gazetteer of this guide is supplied by the participating churches. While this is believed to be correct at the time of going to press, Scotland's Churches Scheme cannot accept any responsibility for its accuracy.

❶ ST ANDREW'S, ARDROSSAN

**South Crescent Road
Ardrossan
KA22 8EA**

⚔ NS 239 420

🏛 Scottish Episcopal

🌐 www.standrews-stpeters.org.uk

Linked with St Andrew's Irvine, St Peter's Dalry

On the seafront.

Simple cruciform church in pink sandstone by David Thomson, 1875, in Early English Gothic style. A rose window above the porch on the west gable and large windows in the transepts light the interior with its elaborate timber crossing. Stained glass: Crucifixion by J. E. W. Guthrie and *Angel plucking Tulips* by Harrington Mann. Allen digital organ.

- Sunday: 11.15am; Wednesday: 10.00am
- Open by arrangement (01294 464968)

❷ ST PETER IN CHAINS, ARDROSSAN

**1 South Crescent
Ardrossan
KA22 8DU**

⚔ NS 233 421

🏛 Roman Catholic

🌐 www.saintpeterinchains.net

Linked with St Winin's Kilwinning

Designed by Jack Coia and opened in 1938, St Peter in Chains is probably the most academic of this period. The church, in reddish facing brick, has a high west gable as at St Columba, Hopehill Road, Glasgow and a tower to the right reminiscent of Stockholm Town Hall. Striking brick main doorway with stone keystone; the door feature continues to the gable roof and ends in a small well-detailed cross.

- Monday to Saturday Mass: 9.30am, 7.00pm; Saturday Vigil Mass: 6.30pm; Sunday: 10.00am, 12.00 noon and 6.30pm
- Open daily 9.00am–7.30pm

Ⓐ 👂

3 BRODICK CHURCH

**Knowe Road
Brodick
Arran
KA27 8BY**

NS 011 360
Church of Scotland

Linked with Corrie

1.6km (1 mile) north of pier, turn left at sports park.

The present church was built in 1910 from local red sandstone. The pulpit, built by local craftsmen, is an exact replica of John Knox's pulpit. Two stained glass windows are in memory of church member Bethia Torrance who died in 1958. Originally the church hall was Bennecarrigan Free Church on the west side of the island. Since it was no longer in use it was transported in March 1950 alongside Brodick Church as a hall.

- Sunday: 10.30am
- Open by arrangement (01770 302248)

4 CHURCH OF THE HOLY CROSS, BRODICK

**Douglas Hotel Grounds
Brodick
Arran
KA27 8AJ**

NS 015 359
Roman Catholic

This beautiful little red sandstone building dates from the 1850s. Rectangular with round-headed windows and a Celtic cross finial on the east gable. It was later used as the Arran Courthouse and for other functions. The interior was recast in 1982 and the building reconsecrated in 1983. Carved altar by Canon Gillies of Arisaig.

- Summer – Saturday Vigil Mass: 7.30pm; Sunday Mass: 9.30am and 11.00am; Winter – Sunday Mass: 11.00am
- Open by arrangement (01770 302030)

NORTH AYRSHIRE

5 CORRIE CHURCH

**Corrie
Arran
KA27 8JB**

🏛 NS 024 437
⛪ Church of Scotland

Linked with Brodick

9.7km (6 miles) north of Brodick.

Designed by J. J. Burnet 1887 as 'one of a family of long, low friendly churches'. Constructed in red sandstone in Early Gothic style with a simple stone belfry and wooden porch. An unusual baptismal font is set into the arch and church wall and rush-bottomed chairs take the place of pews. Lit by circular candelabra. Two tapestries by Mrs Sandeman and two recently installed stained glass windows by Richard Leclerc.

- Sunday: 12.00 noon
- Opening times on church door or by arrangement (01770 810210)

6 KILMORY PARISH CHURCH

**Kilmory
Arran
KA27 8PQ**

🏛 NR 700 449
⛪ Church of Scotland

Turn right after Creamery on road from Whiting Bay.

Present church built 1880 over the previous building of 1765. Small, delightful hall church with Gothic details. Plain windows surrounded by red-coloured stained glass provide a warm ambience.

- Sunday: 10.00am
- Open by arrangement (01770 870305)

7 LAMLASH PARISH CHURCH

Shore Road, Lamlash
Arran
KA27 8NP

🗺 NS 026 309

⛪ Church of Scotland

🌐 homepage.ntlworldcom/morritek/
lamlashchurch/index.htm

A massive campanile tower over 27m (90ft) high sits above this Gothic-style, red sandstone building by H. & D. Barclay 1886. The church was built by 12th Duke of Hamilton to replace an earlier building of 1773. Boarded, barrel-vaulted ceiling and carved, wooden tripartite Gothic sedilia. The tower hosts a peal of nine bells played every Sunday before service, the largest peal still existing, cast for a Scottish church in a Scottish foundry. Seven stained glass windows by Anning Bell, Meiklejohn, Gordon Webster and Christian Shaw; all other windows are hand-painted, German cathedral glass. Pipe organ, William Hill, Norman & Beard 1934. In the front grounds are an ancient cross and baptismal font from the old monastery on Holy Isle in Lamlash Bay. Major restoration programme begun 1997.

- Sunday: 11.30am
- Open by arrangement (01770 600975)

8 ST BRIDE'S, LOCHRANZA

Lochranza
Arran
KA27 8HJ

🗺 NR 937 503

⛪ Church of Scotland

Linked with Pirnmill, St Molio's Shiskine

At T-junction in centre of Lochranza.

The present church was rebuilt in 1712 on the site of the previous church of 1654. A beautiful, simple and attractive church featuring a circular stained glass window in the east gable depicting the Ship of the Gospel sailing through the troubled Sea of Life. This window and the unusual lychgate were given by Miss Edith Kerr in memory of the Rev. John Colville, minister here 1922–31.

- Sunday: 9.30am
- Key available from Lochranza Field Centre (01770 830637), or by arrangement (01770 830222)

9 PIRNMILL CHURCH

Pirnmill
Arran
KA27 8HP

A NR 873 443

Church of Scotland

Linked with St Bride's Lochranza, St Molios Shiskine

On main street, at the north end of the village.

Known locally as 'The Tin Kirk', the building previously belonged to the Free Church of Scotland. A small and friendly congregation which warmly invites visitors to join them for worship. Access is by a footpath through a field – it looks worse than it is!

• Sunday: 10.45am
• Open by arrangement (01770 302334)

10 ST MOLIOS, SHISKINE

Shiskine
Arran
KA27 8EP

A NR 910 295

Church of Scotland

Linked with St Bride's Lochranza, Pirnmill

On B880, 1.6km (1 mile) north of junction with A841.

Known locally as 'The Red Kirk' because the local Machrie sandstone of its construction is of a warm, red hue, this church was built in 1889 to a design by J. J. Burnet. The tower contains a single bell. Set into the west wall of the tower is a carved stone graveslab, possibly of a 13th-century abbot taken from Clauchen graveyard. The north gable has a double window in Norman style with Celtic motifs. A small wooden carving of St Molios, who lived as a hermit on Holy Island, is set into a bench end on the south side of the sanctuary.

• Sunday: 12.00 noon
• Open daily

 (Thursday 10.00am–1200 noon)

11 WHITING BAY & KILDONAN CHURCH

Sandbraes
Whiting Bay
Arran
KA27 8RE

NS 047 273
Church of Scotland

T-plan simple Gothic church with a tall square tower, 1910, built of red-harled brick with red sandstone margins. The tower was restored in 2008. Stained glass windows designed by Christian Shaw depicting the four seasons were added in 1997. The west transept serves as a preschool nursery weekday mornings; the east transept for informal services.

- Sunday: 10.30am all year, and 6.30pm on 3rd Sunday of month
- Open by arrangement (01770 700626 or 01770 700289)

 (rear door)

12 ST MARGARET OF SCOTLAND, WHITING BAY

Whiting Bay
Arran
KA27 8RE

NS 047 273
Scottish Episcopal
www.scotland-anglican.org/argyll

On main road at north end of Whiting Bay.

Built c.1960 for the Free Church; acquired (after a period as a holiday home) with a legacy from Elsie Wood, widow of Canon Charles Wood; dedicated 1995. Friendly ambience. Stained glass window by Eilidh Keith of Glasgow. Eagle lectern from St Andrew's-on-the-Green, Glasgow, and a Slavonic (possibly Serbian) icon.

- Sunday: 11.00am Holy Communion (1970 Liturgy on 2nd Sunday); Evensong 4th Sunday: 6.00pm March to September, 3.00pm October to February
- Open by arrangement (01770 700225)

13 BEITH HIGH CHURCH

**Kirk Road
Beith
KA15 1EX**

A NS 350 539

Church of Scotland

www.beithparishchurches.co.uk

Linked with Beith Trinity

Built in 1807 and extended in 1885. Gothic T-plan kirk dominated by the tall five-stage tower. Panelled gallery on three sides supported on cast-iron columns. Marble and onyx baptismal font, 1896. Stained glass by Gordon Webster. Harrison & Harrison pipe organ in Gothic case, 1885.

- Sunday: 10.30am. Joint service with Beith Trinity during the month of August
- Open by arrangement (01505 502686)

14 BEITH TRINITY CHURCH

**Wilson Street
Beith
KA15 2BE**

A NS 351 544

Church of Scotland

www.beithparishchurches.co.uk

Linked with Beith High

Built 1883, architect Robert Baldie. The chief external feature is a graceful octagonal tower. Interior destroyed by fire 1917, rebuilt 1926. Gothic style, with rectangular nave, Gothic arched chancel and one transept on the east side. Stained glass by John C. Hall & Co. Organ 1937 by Hill, Norman & Beard.

- Sunday: 11.00am. Joint service with Beith High during the month of July
- Open by arrangement (01505 502131)

CATHEDRAL OF THE ISLES, MILLPORT

**College Street, Millport
Cumbrae
KA28 0HE**

NS 166 552

Scottish Episcopal

www.argyllandtheisles.org.uk/cumbrae.html

An important Tractarian church commissioned by the 6th Earl of Glasgow. Cathedral, college and cloister by William Butterfield 1851, one of the masters of the Gothic revival. The nave and chancel is supported by a massive tower and spire. Bright and colourful stencilwork in the chancel designed by Butterfield, stained glass by William Wailes and Hardman. Peal of bells, organ. Visitors welcome to picnic in the grounds.

- Sunday: 11.00am Sung Eucharist; other times see notice-board in porch
- Open daily

CUMBRAE PARISH CHURCH

**Bute Terrace
Millport
Cumbrae
KA28 0BD**

NS 160 550

Church of Scotland

The church, with battlemented tower, pinnacles and clock, was erected in 1837. There are two very interesting grotesques, from the old Kirkton Church, in the chancel, also a lintel with inscribed Hebrew lettering.

- Sunday: 11.00am
- Open by arrangement (01475 530393)

NORTH AYRSHIRE

17 ST MARGARET'S PARISH CHURCH, DALRY

**The Cross
Dalry
KA24 5AL**

A NS 291 496

Church of Scotland

www.btinternet.com/
st.margaretschurch

Landmark Victorian Gothic building (David Thomson 1871–3). Inventive 48.5m (159ft) broach spire 'worthy of the many tasks thrust upon it'; the whole building is a 'powerful, carefully handled composition'. The restored interior (with good acoustics) of the early 1950s presents 'a space of deep solemnity enhanced' by Beith-made pulpit, table, lectern and stained glass by Guthrie & Wells, Charles Payne and C. L. Davidson, plus the only decent amount of Munich glass and only Francis Hemony bell (1661) in a UK church. Three-manual Blackett & Howden organ (1899) moved here in 1953. Communion silver of 1618. Bronze sundial and some interesting stones in kirkyard. Kirk bears the name of the original medieval dedication: St Margaret of Antioch (see modern Rona Moody window), the only such in Scotland.

- Sunday: 10.30am
- Open by arrangement (01294 833135)

18 ST PETER'S, DALRY

**Tofts
Dalry
KA24 5AS**

A NS 297 495

Scottish Episcopal

www.standrews-stpeters.org.uk

Linked with St Andrew's Irvine, St Andrew's Ardrossan

On north side of A737.

This pretty little church was constructed in 1889. The present interior dates from 1978 when a part of the main church was partitioned to provide a vestry / meeting room. St Peter's is firmly rooted in the Scottish Episcopal tradition and part of the North Ayrshire team ministry.

- Sunday: 10.00am
- Open by arrangement (01294 833294)

FAIRLIE CHURCH

**Main Road
Fairlie
KA29 0AD**

⚔ NS 210 560

⛪ Church of Scotland

🌐 www.fairlieparish.co.uk

Chapel of Ease of 1834, taking its present strong traditional form in 1883 with the addition of the chancel, transepts and tower by J. J. Stevenson. The weather vane is a model of the 1920s Fife racing yacht *Latifa* (the yachts were designed and built in Fairlie). The 9th / 10th-century Fairlie Stone is displayed within the church. Excellent stained glass by Morris & Co and Heaton, Butler & Bayne.

- Sunday: 10.30am all year; Thursday: 10.00am September to May
- Open Thursday 10.00am–12 noon for Fairtrade Kirk Café

 **IRVINE OLD PARISH CHURCH**

**Kirkgate
Irvine
KA12 0DF**

⚔ NS 322 387

⛪ Church of Scotland

🌐 www.irvineold.co.uk

The church, 1774 by David Muir, is the third to occupy the site. A large classical building with round-headed windows lighting the gallery. The clock in the six-stage octagonal steeple was presented by Irvine Volunteers in 1803. The stained glass windows are a fine example of Keir brothers work. The graveyard contains fine classical monuments.

- Sunday: 11.00am
- Open by arrangement (01294 279265)

21 ST ANDREW'S PARISH CHURCH, IRVINE

**Ferguson Memorial
Caldon Road
Irvine
KA12 0RF**

Ⓐ NS 325 399

Church of Scotland

Scottish Episcopal

🌐 www.standrews-stpeters.org

Linked with St Andrew's Ardrossan,
St Peter's Dalry

Junction with Oaklands Avenue.

St Andrew's was gifted in 1957 to commemorate the centenary of the death of John Ferguson, founder of the Ferguson bequest. Architect Rennie & Bramble of Saltcoats. Stained glass windows by Mary Wood 1957, Ann Marie Docherty 1998 and Stained Glass Design Partnership of Milngavie 2000. The congregation shares the church with the local Scottish Episcopalian congregation who built on a chapel / meeting room, containing tapestry by Vampboulles, and coffee lounge in 1981. Architect R. L. Dunlop of Troon.

- Sunday: Scottish Episcopal 9.30am; Church of Scotland 11.15am
- Open by arrangement (01294 276413)

22 FULLARTON PARISH CHURCH, IRVINE

**Church Street
Irvine
KA12 8QJ**

Ⓐ NS 316 389

Church of Scotland

🌐 www.fullartonchurch.co.uk

Marress Roundabout.

Built 1838 and designed by Ingram of Kilmarnock. School of 1640 now forms part of the halls. Vestry of 1907. Two stained glass windows of 1958 by G. Maille & Son of London depicting *The Good Shepherd* and *Christ Blessing Little Children* in memory of the Rev. John Paterson, much-loved Minister from 1903–37. Memorial to James Montgomery, Christian poet and hymn writer. Digital organ by the Bradford Computing Organ Co. 1994.

- Sunday: 11.00am
- Open by arrangement (01294 273741)

Ⓑ

23 GIRDLE TOLL CHURCH, IRVINE

**Bryce Knox Court
Girdle Toll
Irvine
KA11 2BJ**

Å NS 342 408

Church of Scotland

⊕ www.girdletoll.fsbusiness.co.uk

Octagonal church of 1992, designed by Ian Hepburn, fitting neatly into the yard of a traditional farm steading. The farm buildings have been converted to accommodate halls and the farmhouse the manse. Harled walls and a slate roof provide a vernacular touch.

- Sunday: 11.00am
- Open Tuesday 10.00am–12 noon in winter, other times by arrangement (01294 215560)

24 THE AULD KIRK OF KILBIRNIE

**Dalry Road
Kilbirnie
KA25 6HY**

Å NS 315 536

Church of Scotland

⊕ www.kilbirnieauldkirk.org.uk

Junction of B780 and B777.

A pre-Reformation church on the site of 6th-century cell dedicated to St Brendan of Clonfert. The nave dates from 1470 and the bell-tower from 1490. Magnificent interior with splendid aisles and lofts: Glengarnock aisle added 1597, pulpit c.1620, and Crawfurd aisle added 1642 all with unique Renaissance-style carving.

- Sunday: 11.00am September to June, 10.00am July and August
- Open July and August, Tuesday, Wednesday and Thursday 2.00–4.00pm, or by arrangement (01505 683878)

 (in halls)

25 ST COLUMBA'S, KILBIRNIE

**Glasgow Street
Kilbirnie
KA25 7AP**

A NS 314 546

Church of Scotland

The old church was built in 1843 and reconstructed and enlarged 1903. The design of a sloping floor and balcony is unusual. The balcony front is French Fibre plasterwork. Table runner by Malcolm Lochhead. Three-light window by Stephen Adam in the hall which is the former Kilbirnie West Church.

- Sunday: 11.15am
- Open by arrangement (01505 683342)

26 ABBEY CHURCH, KILWINNING

**Main Street
Kilwinning
KA13 7RU**

A NS 303 433

Church of Scotland

Built in 1774 by John Garland and John Wright with the tower by David Hamilton, 1815. The church is on the site of the ruined abbey, founded in 1188, and replaced the first Reformation church built in 1590. The organ built by Foster & Anderson of Hull was first played in 1897 and is highly regarded. The church has strong links with the Earls of Eglinton.

- Sunday: 9.15am and 11.00am September to May; 10.00am June to August
- Open by arrangement (01294 552929)

27 ERSKINE CHURCH, KILWINNING

**Garden Square Lane
Kilwinning
KA13 6AN**

NS 303 434

Church of Scotland

Linked with Fergushill Kilwinning

Off Main Street.

Simple United Presbyterian-style building, 1838, down a lane from Main Street. Pedimented open bellcote flanked by projecting brackets. Gables neatly finished with small finials. Pleasant restored interior with gallery.

- Sunday: 11.30am
- Open by arrangement (01294 554376)

28 FERGUSHILL CHURCH, KILWINNING

**17 Woodburn Avenue
Benslie Village
Kilwinning
KA13 7DB**

NS 337 430

Church of Scotland

Linked with Erskine Kilwinning

Church extension for the mining community from Kilwinning Parish Church built in 1879 to a plan prepared by William Railton of Kilmarnock. Attractive church with bell-tower. Fine views to Arran.

- Sunday: 10.00am
- Open by arrangement (01294 850257)

NORTH AYRSHIRE

29 ST WININ'S, KILWINNING

St Winning's Lane
Kilwinning
KA13 6EP

NS 300 432

Roman Catholic

www.st-winins.org.uk

Linked with St Peter's Ardrossan

The modern Catholic Parish was founded in 1871 and was served by a priest from Dalry, a neighbouring parish. The present church was built in 1937 and replaced a chapel school of around 1872, now the hall. The church interior was reordered in 1997 and now seats 400 and is well-used by the 700 or 800 congregation who attend weekend masses.

- Saturday: 6.30pm; Sunday: 10.00am and 12.00 noon
- Open by arrangement (01294 552276)

 (side door) (in halls)

30 MANSEFIELD TRINITY CHURCH, KILWINNING

West Doura Way
Stevenston Road
Kilwinning
KA13 6DY

NS 290 432

Church of Scotland

www.mansefieldtrinitychurch.co.uk

The first church opened by the Church of Scotland in the new millennium. Designed by architects James F. Stephens, the building has a distinctive round design, which creates a light and airy atmosphere. Floor-to-ceiling windows allow the church to be flooded with sunlight during services throughout the year. The building is multipurpose and reflects current thinking, being open and accessible.

- Sunday: 11.00am October to June, 10.30am July to September
- Open 10.00am–2.00pm Tuesday and Thursday, or by arrangement (01294 550746)

31 CLARK MEMORIAL CHURCH, LARGS

**Bath Street
Largs
KA30 8BL**

NS 202 593

Church of Scotland

Gifted by John Clark of the Anchor Thread Mills, Paisley, and designed by William Kerr of T. G. Abercrombie, Paisley 1892. Red sandstone from Locharbriggs and Corsehill in Early English Gothic style with a rich interior. Superb stained glass, all manufactured in Glasgow at height of Arts & Crafts movement. Hammer-beam roof. Organ by 'Father' Willis 1892. Views of the Clyde and Cumbraes.

- Sunday: 10.00am; Thursday: 10.30am
- Viking Festival one week each September
- Open daily 10.00am–4.00pm (except Tuesdays)

32 ST COLUMBA'S PARISH CHURCH, LARGS

**Gallowgate
Largs
KA30 8LX**

NS 203 596

Church of Scotland

www.largscolumba.com

The old parish church was replaced by the present building in 1892. It is a handsome structure by architects Henry Steele and Andrew Balfour, of red stone with a 3-stage tower with spire and clock. Interesting carved octagonal oak pulpit and notable windows. 'Father' Willis organ 1892, generally regarded as one of the finest church instruments in Scotland. Memorial to General Sir Thomas MacDougall Brisbane, astronomer, soldier and Governor of New South Wales.

- Sunday: 11.00am
- Open 10.00am–12.00 noon, Monday to Friday

  (by arrangement)

  (Saturdays, June to September)

33 ST COLUMBA'S, LARGS

**Aubery Crescent
Largs
KA30 8PR**

A   NS 201 603

Scottish Episcopal

⊕   www.geocities.com/largschurch

Built in 1876 on land gifted by the Brisbane family, and the construction funded by the Earl of Glasgow. Charming and delicate exercise in the Early English style by Ross and McBeth of Inverness. Victorian stained glass, including a rose window depicting a dove, symbol of the Holy Spirit and St Columba. Memorials to the Brisbane and Boyle (Earls of Glasgow) families and to the scientist Lord Kelvin. Embroidered kneelers made for the centenary.

- Sunday: 8.00am, 11.00am, 6.30pm; Wednesday: 10.00am
- Open 9.00am–5.00pm daily, except Friday

34 ST JOHN'S, LARGS

**Bath Street
Largs
KA30 8BL**

A   NS 201 593

Church of Scotland

⊕   www.stjohnslargs.co.uk

Built as a Free Church in 1843 and named St John's in 1900 after union of the Free and United Presbyterian Churches. Designed by A. J. Graham, the building is in the Romanesque style with the tall tower at the north-west corner and vestry to the south-west linked by an arcaded narthex.

- Sunday: 11.00am and 6.30pm
- Open by arrangement (01475 686729)

ST MARY'S STAR OF THE SEA, LARGS

**28 Greenock Road
Largs
KA30 8NE**

 NS 203 599

Roman Catholic

www.stmaryslargs.co.uk

A bright modern building opened in 1962. The architect was Mr A. R. Conlon of Reginald Fairlie & Sons. Features include a tapestry at the High Altar depicting Jesus and two disciples at Emmaus, eight stained glass panels above the main door, and a statue outside the main door of Our Lady, Star of the Sea, by eminent Scottish sculptor, Hew Lorimer.

- Saturday Vigil: 6.30pm; Sunday: 9.00am and 11.30am
- Open 8.30am–8.00pm in summer, 8.30am–3.30pm in winter

 **ST CUTHBERT'S PARISH CHURCH, SALTCOATS**

**13 Caledonia Road
Saltcoats
KA21 5AP**

NS 244 418

Church of Scotland

www.stcuthbertssaltcoats.com

Designed by Peter MacGregor Chalmers and dedicated in 1908, the fourth building of the congregation of Ardrossan Parish. The chancel displays a marble reredos of the Last Supper. Sixteen stained glass windows on the life of Christ by William Wilson 1947; two windows by Gordon Webster 1976. Model of a French frigate of 1804, by sailor William Dunlop, hangs in the church. He made it as a thanksgiving for his surviving the Napoleonic Wars when a cannonball narrowly missed his hammock.

- Sunday: 11.15am
- Open by arrangement (01294 466636)

37 ST BRENDAN'S, SALTCOATS

**63 Corrie Crescent
Saltcoats
KA21 6JN**

A NS 247 430
Roman Catholic
www.rcsaltcoats.com

St Brendan's was designed in the contemporary style of the 1960s. It is surrounded by a raised foot-walk and has a spacious narthex which is separated from the nave by a glass screen decorated with ironwork. Altar and pulpit of Connemara marble. Magnificent contemporary stained glass window depicting the life of St Brendan the Navigator and a unique crucifix, designed locally and fabricated in steel.

• Saturday: 6.30pm; Sunday: 11.00am
• Open by arrangement (01294 463483)

38 NEW TRINITY PARISH CHURCH, SALTCOATS

**Chapelwell Street
Saltcoats
KA21 5EA**

A NS 246 414
Church of Scotland
www.newtrinity.co.uk

Congregation formed by the union of Erskine and Landsborough Trinity Churches in 1993. The former Erskine Church buildings of 1866 are used. The building, designed by William Stewart, has a spire and pinnacles above a polychrome Venetian Gothic façade. Additional halls built 1970. Organ, Forster & Andrews 1899. Four stained glass windows depicting *Music, The Good Shepherd, Dorcas* and *The Sower of the Seed.*

• Sunday: 11.15am; Thursday: 10.30am
• Open by arrangement (01294 602410)

39 SKELMORLIE & WEMYSS BAY CHURCH

**Shore Road
Skelmorlie
PA17 5DR**

Ⓐ NS 192 681

Church of Scotland

www.skelmorliechurch.org.uk

Gothic church with nave and chancel and a square tower, built 1895 and designed by John Honeyman to replace a 'chapel of ease' of 1856. Free-standing wrought-iron lamp by Charles Rennie Mackintosh, 1895, at the entrance. Stained glass by Douglas Strachan (*Stilling the Storm*), Stephen Adam, Edward Burne Jones and Charles E. Kempe. Organ by Binns 1910.

- Sunday: 11.00am
- Open Saturdays July and August 2.00–4.00pm, or by arrangement (01475 520703)

 B (church) A (lamp)

40 ST JOHN'S, STEVENSTON

**Hayocks Road
Stevenson
KA20 4DE**

Ⓐ NS 271 421

Roman Catholic

www.stjohnsrc.force9.co.uk

Built 1963 to designs by James B. G. Houston. Features laminated trusses supporting the roof and beautiful stained glass by M. Gabriel Loire of Chartres representing biblical scenes and St John the Evangelist. Brass baptismal font depicting a half tree-trunk sheltering a fawn: 'As the deer longs for streams of water, so my soul yearns for you, my God.'

- Saturday Vigil: 6.30pm; Sunday: 11.00am, weekdays 10am (subject to change)
- Open by arrangement (01294 463225)

41 OVERTON CHURCH, WEST KILBRIDE

Ritchie Street
West Kilbride
KA23 9AL

NS 203 481

Church of Scotland

www.overtonchurch.co.uk

Boldly detailed French Gothic church designed by Hippolyte Le Blanc in 1883. Very good stained glass with two recent modern additions. Two-manual Binns Organ – tubular pneumatic. Unusual hipped wooden ceiling to nave.

- Sunday: 11.00am all year, occasional 6.30pm evening service
- Open by arrangement (01294 822368)

 (by arrangement)

 (Thursday morning)

42 ST ANDREW'S, WEST KILBRIDE

Main Street
West Kilbride
KA23 9AW

NS 207 484

Church of Scotland

200m (656ft) from railway station.

Built as St Bride's United Presbyterian Church in 1882, in typical UP style of red sandstone with a fine spire and rose window. In 1972 it united with the Barony Parish, changing its name to St Andrew's. Allen Digital organ 1983.

- Sunday: 10.30am contemporary in upper room, or traditional in sanctuary; 3.00pm on 1st Sunday traditional
- Open Monday to Friday 9.30am–12.30pm (enter from the lane at the side of the church)

43 ST BRIDE'S, WEST KILBRIDE

**9 Hunterston Road
West Kilbride
KA23 9EX**

 NS 206 484

Roman Catholic

The church was built and opened in 1908. The Marian shrine in the grounds was erected in 1958 for the Golden Jubilee.

- Saturday Vigil: 6.30pm; Sunday: 10.30am; weekdays (including Saturdays) 9.30am
- Open daily 9.00am–6.00pm

44 AUCHINLECK PARISH CHURCH

**Church Hill
Auchinleck
KA18 2AB**

NS 552 216

Church of Scotland

Linked with Catrine

There has been a church on this site since the 12th century. The present building, designed by James Ingram, was begun in 1833 and was funded by the Boswell family. The bell-tower, designed by Robert Ingram, was added 1897. The interior was completely rebuilt after a fire in 1938. Organ by Hill, Norman & Beard. James Chrystal, a Moderator of the General Assembly of the Church of Scotland, served as Minister for over sixty years. In the churchyard is the Boswell Aisle of 1754.

- Sunday: 11.15am
- Open by arrangement (01290 422946)

45 CATRINE PARISH CHURCH

**Chapel Brae
Catrine
KA5 6QS**

🏛 NS 528 260

🏠 Church of Scotland

Linked with Auchinleck

B713, 4.8km (3 miles) east of Mauchline.

Charming church, built as a chapel of ease in 1792, financed by Sir Claud Alexander of Ballochmyle. It was established as a parish church when Catrine was made a quoad sacra parish in 1871. The church is dignified by refined classical details and a central pediment topped with the belfry. Major renovations in 1874, 1960, 1992 and 2003. Stained glass. Harrison & Harrison pipe organ 1883. Overlooking Catrine in the River Ayr valley.

- Sunday: 10.00am
- Open by arrangement (01290 551601)

46 CROSSHOUSE PARISH CHURCH

**25 Kilmarnock Road
Crosshouse
KA2 0EX**

🏛 NS 395 384

🏠 Church of Scotland

🌐 www.crosshouseparishchurch.
org.uk

Designed by Bruce & Sturrock, the church was built 1882 in red sandstone with an 18m (60ft) steeple over the front door. Stained glass windows on all sides with a rose window on the rear elevation. Traditional layout to seat 500. Manual pipe organ with pedal board in the chancel has a beautiful sound. The church is the focal point of the parish.

- Sunday: 11.00am
- Open weekends and by arrangement (01563 535975)

47 OLD CUMNOCK OLD CHURCH

**The Square
Cumnock
KA18 1DB**

 NS 568 202

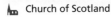 Church of Scotland

⊕ www.e-ayrshire.co.uk/local/
oldcumnock

Commanding a prominent position in the square of this old market town, the church was built in 1866 through the patronage of the Marquess of Bute. The Bute family seats remain in the Memorial Chapel. Organ 1966. Mosaic of Jesus walking on the water by James Harrigan. Bell in vestibule was cast in 1697 by Quinus de Vesscher of Rotterdam, and was used in the two churches which preceded the present building.

- Sunday: 11.30am, on days of opening 12.30pm; Friday: 12.30pm
- Open July and August, Tuesday and Friday 12.00 noon–4.00pm, Thursday 11.00am–2.00pm

     (not Wednesdays)

48 ST JOHN THE EVANGELIST, CUMNOCK

**92 Glaisnock Road
Cumnock
KA18 1JU**

 NS 572 196

Roman Catholic

Linked with St Thomas Muirkirk

Rare Scottish example of the work of William Burges, 1882, for the Marquess of Bute, and the first ecclesiastical building in Scotland to be lit by electricity. Lush feast of painted surfaces, rich furniture, glorious stained glass and an altarpiece by J. F. Bentley and N. J. Westlake.

- Saturday: 6.00pm; Sunday: 11.45am
- Open by arrangement (01290 421031)

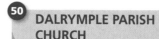

49 CUMNOCK CONGREGATIONAL CHURCH

**4 Auchinleck Road
Cumnock
KA18 1AE**

A NS 566 203

⌂ Congregational

⊕ www.cumnockcongregational.
co.uk

The church began with twelve members in 1838. The present building is situated beside the River Lugar at the entrance to Woodroad Park. This friendly, compact sandstone church was dedicated in 1883. The first Labour Member of Parliament, Keir Hardie, served on the Diaconate. Impressive two-manual organ with eleven ranks of pipes.

- Sunday: 11.00am and 6.30pm September to June, 10.30am July and August
- Open by arrangement (01290 421982)

50 DALRYMPLE PARISH CHURCH

**Church Street
Dalrymple
KA6 6DQ**

A NS 358 145

⌂ Church of Scotland

⊕ www.ayrpresbytery.co.uk

Linked with Crosshill

Vernacular stone-built, slate-roofed church built in 1850 to replace a building allegedly frequented by Robert Burns. Vestry and session house added 1964. Large west window and one north window, 1900, by acclaimed Scottish stained glass artist Stephen Adams. Organ, also 1900, by Stovell and Lewis of Edinburgh.

- Sunday: 10.30am
- Open by arrangement (01292 560194)

51 DARVEL PARISH CHURCH

**Hastings Square
Darvel
KA17 0DR**

Ⰱ NS 563 375

Ⰱ Church of Scotland

The church is prominently set in the centre of the village square, adjacent to the memorial to Sir Alexander Fleming, the discoverer of penicillin. Designed by Robert S. Ingram and built 1887–8 in Early English style with a tower and spire 40m (130ft) high. The Sanctuary has a nave, transept, aisles and a back gallery with woodwork of pitch pine. The pulpit of carved oak is particularly handsome and incorporates a Forster & Andrews pipe organ and backed by a triple lancet stained glass window. In the east wall is the Morton of Gowanbank memorial stained glass window of 1958.

- Sunday: 11.00am
- Open by arrangement (01560 322924)

**52 OUR LADY OF THE
VALLEY, DARVEL**

**4 West Donington Street
Darvel
KA17 0AP**

Ⰱ NS 563 374

Ⰱ Roman Catholic

🌐 www.saintsophias.com

Linked with St Sophia's Galston, St Paul's Hurlford

Church built by seceders in 1874 and closed in 1927. Various users of the building, e.g. Girl Guides, until early 1950s when it again lay empty. Purchased in mid-1960s by Darvel Parish Church and used as a church hall before being sold to the Catholic community and opened by Bishop Maurice Taylor on 25 November 1984.

- Wednesday: 10.00am; Saturday: 10.00am
- Open by arrangement (01560 320346)

53 **ST CLARE'S, DRONGAN**

Watson Terrace
Drongan
KA6 7AB

NS 441 185

Roman Catholic

Linked with St Paul's Ayr, St Francis Waterside

1.6km (1 mile) south of A70, 11.3km (7 miles) east of Ayr.

Unassuming church building opened in 1967. The interior is given drama by the roof light which brings light flooding onto the altar.

- Sunday: 9.45am
- Open by arrangement (01292 260197)

WC

54 **DUNLOP PARISH CHURCH**

Main Street
Dunlop
KA3 4AG

NS 405 494

Church of Scotland

A Christian site since the 13th century, the present church dates from 1835, though the sculptured stonework of the Dunlop Aisle, 1641, was preserved. Magnificent collection of stained glass by Gordon Webster. Beside the church is Clandeboyes Hall, 1641, built as a school. Built onto the back of Clandeboyes is the early 17th-century monumental tomb of Hans Hamilton, first Protestant minister of Dunlop.

- Sunday: 11.00am
- Open Sunday 2.00–4.00pm, June to September

B (church) **A** (hall and tomb)

55 FENWICK PARISH CHURCH

Kirkton Road
Fenwick
KA3 6DH

NS 465 435

Church of Scotland

Built 1643 in the shape of a Greek cross, with four arms of equal length. Features of note include outside stairs to Rowallan loft with the coat of arms of the Mures of Rowallan above the door, crowstepped gables and 'the jougs' on the south wall. Several Covenanting artefacts, including the battleflag of the Fenwick Covenanters. Walled graveyard contains several notable graves and monuments.

- Sunday: 11.00am
- Open by arrangement (01560 600217)

     (in halls)

56 GALSTON PARISH CHURCH

Cross Street
Galston
KA4 8AL

NS 500 367

Church of Scotland

www.galstonparish.org.uk

Present church, designed by John Brash of Glasgow, erected 1809 on site of Christian worship since 1252. Third church since Reformation. Spire 37m (120ft). Chancel added 1912 and three-manual pipe organ by J. J. Binns 1913. Stained glass windows the work of Oscar Paterson, a contemporary of Charles Rennie Mackintosh. Full restoration of church building completed in 1999. Floodlit since 2000. Ministers include Dr George Smith, great-grandfather of Robert Louis Stevenson and mentioned by Robert Burns in 'The Holy Fair' (grave on north side of church). Also Rev. Robert Stirling, inventor of the Stirling Engine. Gravestone of Andrew Richmond, killed by Graham of Claverhouse, on south porch door along with a memorial to five Covenanters.

- Sunday: 11.00am
- Bicentenary events in 2009
- Open by arrangement (01563 820623)

EAST AYRSHIRE

ST SOPHIA'S, GALSTON

**9 Bentinck Street
Galston
KA4 8HT**

⚔ NS 504 365

⛪ Roman Catholic

🌐 www.saintsophias.com

Linked with Our Lady Darvel, St Paul's Hurlford

Constructed 1885–6, architect Sir Robert Rowand Anderson, the church is a distinctive building freely based on Hagia Sophia in Istanbul. At the behest of Lord Bute, who commissioned the church, Anderson, and possibly Weir Schultz, brought to Galston this dark brick echo of the Byzantine Empire.

- Sunday: 11.30am; Monday: 10.00am
- Open by arrangement (01563 820339)

  (by arrangement)

---

58 **HURLFORD CHURCH**

**10 Main Road
Crookedholm
Hurlford
KA3 6JT**

⚔ NS 454 372

⛪ Church of Scotland

Built in 1857 as Reid Memorial Church, united with Hurlford Kirk in 1995. Gothic-style stone church with octagonal tower with spire on the corner. The pipe organ from Hurlford Kirk, built by Foster & Andrews at a cost of £500 in 1875, was moved – all 1,056 pipes and 2.5 tons – to the present church.

- Sunday: 11.00am
- Open by arrangement (01563 535673)

59 ST PAUL'S CHURCH, HURLFORD

**53 Galston Road
Hurlford
KA1 5HT**

🪦 NS 458 370
⛪ Roman Catholic
🌐 www.saintsophias.com

Linked with Our Lady Darvel, St Sophia's Galston

The church is a yellow brick building dating from the 1850s. Gothic arches feature in the light and bright interior.

- Sunday: 10.30am; Friday: 10.00am
- Open by arrangement (01563 525963)

60 KILMARNOCK OLD HIGH KIRK

**Soulis Street
Kilmarnock
KA3 1AP**

🪦 NS 430 382
⛪ Church of Scotland
🌐 www.old-high-kirk.org.uk

Junction with Church Street.

Kilmarnock's oldest church building built 1732 of local stone by the Hunter Brothers to a design adapted from St Martin-in-the-Fields, London. Austere exterior contrasts with pleasing interior enhanced by unique set of 23 stained glass windows by W. & J. J. Keir, glaziers to Glasgow Cathedral. Graveyard with tombs including John Wilson, publisher of Robert Burns's first book of poems.

- Sunday: 11.00am
- o Tartan Day in April; Burns poetry competition, May; Open Door Event in July. See website for details
- Open by arrangement (01563 526064)

(by arrangement)

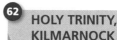

61 LAIGH WEST HIGH KIRK, KILMARNOCK

**John Dickie Street
Kilmarnock
KA1 1BL**

⚔ NS 428 379

⛪ Church of Scotland

🌐 www.lwhk.org.uk

Body of the church by Robert Johnstone 1802. Enlarged 1831 with later 19th-century session room. Major refurbishment 1996 by W. I. Munro Architects, winning 1997 Civic Trust Award for part of town-centre regeneration. Interesting monuments and stained glass. Covenanters' graves in adjacent kirk yard. Close to bus and rail stations.

- Sunday: 11.00am, also 9.30am June to August
- Open Monday, Wednesday, Friday and Saturday 12.00 noon–2.00pm, or by arrangement (01563 528051)

62 HOLY TRINITY, KILMARNOCK

**Portland Road
Kilmarnock
KA1 1EQ**

⚔ NS 426 377

⛪ Scottish Episcopal

🌐 www.holytrinitykilmarnock.co.uk

Junction with Dundonald Road.

The nave was built in 1857 to a design by local architect James Wallace, the chancel and sanctuary were added in 1876 by Sir George Gilbert Scott. Wall and ceiling murals in the chancel, the north ceiling depicts twelve prophets with text scrolls, the south ceiling depicts the twelve apostles and creeds. Mosaic flooring with wheat and grapes. Stained glass in chancel depicts the life of Christ. Pipe organ, 1876, Hill & Sons, with elaborately decorated pipes and fretwork screening, refurbished 1939 by Hill, Norman & Beard.

- Sunday: 9.15am; Holy Communion 11.00am; Sung Eucharist 6.00pm Evensong; Matins 11.00am 1st Sunday, if not a festival
- Usually open daily (01563 523577)

St Ninian's Priory Church, Whithorn   129

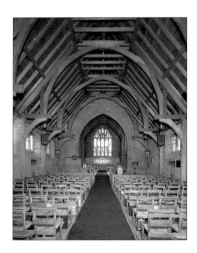

St Ninian's, Troon   111

Lamlash Parish Church   7

Mansefield Trinity Church, Kilwinning   30

Winton Place EU Congregational
Church, Kilmarnock   67

St Andrew's, Moffat   178

Our Lady & St Meddan, Troon   108

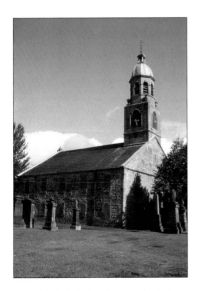

Old High Kirk, Kilmarnock   60   St Peter's Church, Dalbeattie   138

Our Lady & St Meddan, Troon 108

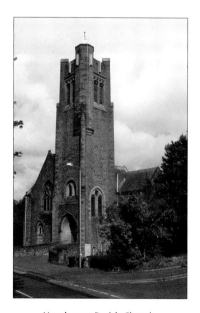

Henderson Parish Church,
Kilmarnock 63

St Peter in Chains, Ardrossan 2

Buittle Parish Church

Cathedral of the Isles, Millport   15

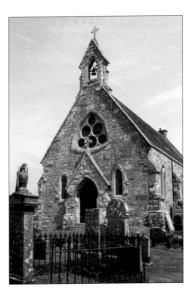

Kilmory Parish Church   6

Kirkmaiden Old Kirk   121

Mouswald

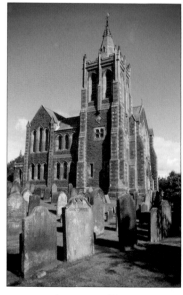

Dryfesdale Parish Church, Lockerbie

All Saints' Church, Challoch   113

Holy Trinity, Lockerbie   177

Lochmaben Church   175

Fenwick Parish Church   55

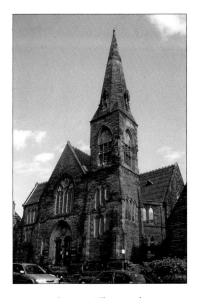

Grange, Kilmarnock   Balmaghie Parish Church

63 HENDERSON PARISH CHURCH, KILMARNOCK

**London Road
Kilmarnock
KA3 7AJ**

⚐ NS 431 380

🏠 Church of Scotland

🌐 www.hendersonchurch.org.uk

Adjacent to Grand Hall, Palace Theatre and bus station.

Brilliantly individual Arts & Crafts treatment of Gothic motifs by Thomas Smellie, Kilmarnock, completed in 1907. Very tall tower above church built on rising ground, with halls below. Carillon of bells 1950. Fine Norman & Beard three-manual organ restored in 1987. Stained glass windows by Gordon Webster, and, in side chapel, by Wendy Robertson 1987. On Burns Heritage Trail, leading to Dean Castle Country Park (open all year).

- Sunday: 9.45am and 11.00am
- o Doors Open Day 1st Sunday in September, open 1.00–4.00pm
- Open by arrangement (01563 528212)

64 OUR LADY OF MOUNT CARMEL, KILMARNOCK

**Kirkton Road
Onthank
Kilmarnock
KA3 2DF**

⚐ NS 428 401

🏠 Roman Catholic

Opened in 1963, Our Lady of Mount Carmel serves the areas of Onthank, Altonhill and Wardneuk in Kilmarnock as well as the villages of Kilmaurs and Fenwick. A large church, possibly its most distinctive features are its stained glass windows and the figure of Christ Crucified.

- Sunday: 9.45am; Thursday: 10.00am
- Open by arrangement (01563 523822)

EAST AYRSHIRE

65 ST MARNOCK'S PARISH CHURCH, KILMARNOCK

**St Marnock Street
Kilmarnock
KA1 1DZ**

Ⅹ NS 427 377

🏠 Church of Scotland

🌐 www.st marnocks.org.uk

In centre of town.

Perpendicular Gothic, rectangular plan six-bay church with centrally placed tower on north gable end, by John Ingram 1836. Fine carillon of bells. Three-manual pipe organ 1872, painted organ screen. Extensive restoration programme completed in 1997.

- Sunday: 11.00am (and 9.30am June to mid-August)
- Open by arrangement (01563 520210)

66 ST MATTHEW'S, KILMARNOCK

**Grassyards Road
Kilmarnock
KA3 7SH**

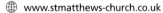

Ⅹ NS 442 388

🏠 Roman Catholic

🌐 www.stmatthews-church.co.uk

The parish of St Matthew's was founded in 1974 to serve the needs of the then developing housing estate in New Farm Loch, Kilmarnock. The church is a modern building built in 1977 to have a dual purpose of both hall and church combined. Built of buff-coloured brick, the interior is lit by a large clerestory window.

- Saturday: 6.30pm; Sunday: 9.30am and 11.00am; Monday, Tuesday, Friday and Saturday: 10.00am; Wednesday: 8.15am
- Open by arrangement (01563 533587)

67 WINTON PLACE EU CONGREGATIONAL CHURCH, KILMARNOCK

Dundonald Road Kilmarnock KA1 1EQ

Ⲗ NS 426 377

ⓐ Congregational Federation

⊕ www.congregational.org/ Kilmarnock

Founder church of the Evangelical Union, started in 1843 by the Rev. James Morrison. The present grey sandstone building, designed by James Ingram, was built in 1860. Three stained glass windows behind the pulpit by Keir of Irvine, 1890, restored 1995.

• Sunday: 11.00am, plus 7.00pm on 1st Sunday of month
• Open by arrangement (01292 313139)

 B WC

68 ST MAUR'S GLENCAIRN PARISH CHURCH

Kilmaurs KA3 2RA

Ⲗ NS 415 408

ⓐ Church of Scotland

On A735.

The church at Kilmaurs was in the possession of Kelso Abbey as early as 1170. In 1413 the present foundation was endowed by Sir William Cunninghame as a collegiate church. Rebuilt by Robert S. Ingram 1888 in a cruciform shape. Stained glass, 20th-century, including a window by Roland Mitton of Livingston, and three rose windows. The clock tower holds the original bell inscribed 'Michael Burgerhuys Me Fecit 1618'. Glencairn Aisle adjacent to the church with sculptured mural 1600 commissioned by James 7th Earl of Glencairn, in memory of the Earl and Countess of Glencairn, and worked by David Scougal, mason and burgess.

• Sunday: 11.00am
• Open by arrangement (01563 538289)

69 MAUCHLINE PARISH CHURCH

**Loudoun Street
Mauchline
KA5 5BT**

⊼ NS 498 272

⛪ Church of Scotland

🌐 www.mauchlineparish.org.uk

Junction of B743 with A76.

Present church by William Alexander 1829 stands on site of St Michael's Church founded in 13th century. Single bell cast in 1742. 'Father' Willis pipe organ 1888 rebuilt in 1980. Associations with Covenanters and Robert Burns, many contemporaries of whom are buried here.

- Sunday: 11.00am
- Mauchline Holy Fair held in late May
- Open by arrangement with Church Officer (01290 552646)

70 ST THOMAS THE APOSTLE, MUIRKIRK

**Wellwood Street
Muirkirk
KA18 3RT**

⊼ NS 699 278

⛪ Roman Catholic

🌐 www.st-thomas-church-muirkirk.org.uk

Linked with St John's Cumnock

Set in beautiful countryside, the village of Muirkirk is a town with an industrial past based on coal, tar and iron. The material for this church, built in 1906, was transported from Belgium.

- Sunday: 10.00am
- Open by arrangement (01290 421031)

71 NEW CUMNOCK PARISH CHURCH

**Castle
New Cumnock
KA18 4AN**

⚲ NS 617 135

 Church of Scotland

🌐 www.newcumnock-parish
church.org.uk

Square church and tower with Gothic details of 1833 by James Ingram built 200m (656ft) from old church (now a ruin). The high pulpit is a feature of the interior which has galleries on three sides. Stained glass windows depicting *Faith, Hope & Charity* are original; the left-hand panel was gifted from Hill Church, Blairgowrie to replace *The Good Shepherd* panel blown out during a storm in the 1940s. Two-manual pipe organ by Hilsdon, 1928. Local Burns connections.

• Sunday: 11.00am
• Open by arrangement (01290 338342)

72 RICCARTON PARISH CHURCH

**Old Street
Riccarton
KA1 4JZ**

⚲ NS 428 364

 Church of Scotland

🌐 www.riccartonparishchurch.co.uk

Classical square-plan church of 1825 by John Richmond with the chancel added in 1910. Beautiful War Memorial window of 1919 in memory of those of the congregation and parish who gave their lives in the Great War. A former Minister, the Rev. Alexander Moodie, mentioned by Burns in 'The Twa Herds' and 'The Holy Fair', is buried in the churchyard.

• Sunday: 11.00am
• Open by arrangement (01563 537982)

EAST AYRSHIRE

73 SORN PARISH CHURCH

**Main Street
Sorn
KA5 6JA**

⚔ NS 550 268
⛪ Church of Scotland

A handsome building standing proudly in its kirkyard, originally built in 1658 and reconstructed in 1826. Improvements made in 1910 by H. E. Clifford. Outside stairs to three galleries. Jougs on the west wall. East wall memorial to George Wood, last Covenanter to die 1688.

• Sunday: 10.00am
• Open by arrangement (01290 551256)

74 OUR LADY AND ST JOHN'S, STEWARTON

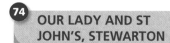

**69 Lainshaw Street
Stewarton
KA3 5BX**

⚔ NS 417 457
⛪ Roman Catholic
🌐 www.e-ayrshire.co.uk/churchof
OurLady

Our Lady and St John's was built in 1974 and functions as church and hall. Modern Stations of the Cross by a local arts teacher.

• Saturday Vigil: 5.00pm; Tuesday: 7.00pm
• Open by arrangement (01560 483322)

75 ST COLUMBA'S PARISH CHURCH, STEWARTON

**1 Kirk Glebe
Stewarton
KA3 5BJ**

NS 419 457

Church of Scotland

Beside the mini-roundabout at the south end of Stewarton.

Built in 1696, renovated in 1775, and widened in 1825 with later additions. Unusual bell-tower above a clock and a rare triangular window. Lainshaw Loft used for smaller services. New and restored windows installed for tercentenary in 1996.

* Sunday: 11.00am
* Open by arrangement (01560 482453)

76 ST FRANCIS XAVIER, WATERSIDE

**Dalmellington Road
Waterside
KA6 7JF**

NS 445 080

Roman Catholic

Linked with St Paul's Ayr, St Clare's Drongan

On A713, 16km (10 miles) south-east of Ayr.

Brick-built church with red sandstone dressings. The church was opened 1895 to cater for the workers of Waterside ironworks. At its peak, the ironworks was one of the largest in Ayrshire and is now being developed as an interpretative centre for the industrial heritage of Ayrshire.

* Saturday Vigil Mass: 6.00pm
* Open by arrangement (01292 260197)

EAST AYRSHIRE

SOUTH AYRSHIRE

 77 ALLOWAY PARISH CHURCH

**Monument Road
Alloway
KA7 4PQ**

⋀ NS 332 181
🏠 Church of Scotland
🌐 www.allowaychurch.org

B7024 south of Burns's cottage.

Built in 1858, architect Campbell Douglas. South transept added in 1877, chancel built and nave extended in 1890. Excellent stained glass including Stephen Adam, Clayton & Bell, Gordon Webster, W. & J. J. Keir. James Crombie memorial window to D. F. McIntyre, pilot on first flight over Mount Everest in 1933. Two windows by Susan Bradbury were installed in 1996, one depicting the four seasons, the other in memory of Robert Burns. Three further Bradbury windows were added in 2001, enhancing the porch and sanctuary area throughout with stained glass.

- Sunday: 9.45am and 11.15am
- Conducted tours, contact local tourist office
- Open June to September, Monday to Friday 10.00am–4.00pm

78 THE AULD KIRK OF AYR

**St John the Baptist
Ayr
KA7 1TT**

⋀ NS 339 219
🏠 Church of Scotland
🌐 www.auldkirk.org

Off the High Street.

The approach to the Auld Kirk is through Kirkport and the 1656 lychgate into the kirkyard. The Commonwealth Government paid for the 1654 T-plan kirk after Cromwell's troops had occupied the old Church of St John on the sands. Respectful alterations by David Bryce of 1836. High-quality interior with three lofts on Corinthian columns and a splendid double-decker pulpit. One of the few remaining 'Obit' boards records money donated to the poor. This church is not a museum, but living and active.

- Sunday: 11.00am
- Open July and August, Saturday 10.30am–12.30pm, or by arrangement (01292 445269)

  (in halls)

79 HOLY TRINITY CHURCH, AYR

Fullarton Street
Ayr
KA7 1UB

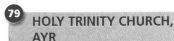

- NS 336 218
- Scottish Episcopal
- www.episcopalsouthayrshire.org.uk

Linked with St Oswald's Maybole, St John's Girvan

Next to Ayr bus station.

Dedicated in 1888. Scotland's major example of the work of J. L. Pearson, designer of Truro Cathedral. Pulpit of Caen stone and very fine stained glass windows by, among others, Clayton & Bell.

- Sunday: 8.00am, 10.30am and 6.30pm; Wednesday: Eucharist 11.00am
- Concert series
- Open mornings in summer

(by arrangement)

80 ST ANDREW'S PARISH CHURCH, AYR

39 Park Circus
Ayr
KA7 2DL

- NS 338 212
- Church of Scotland
- www.standrewsayr.org.uk

South side of the town between the railway and the seafront.

St Andrew's, identified by its tall red sandstone spire, was opened in November 1893. The worshipping congregation came from the Wallacetown Free Church disruption. The design, by John B. Wilson, is Perpendicular Gothic. The beautiful stained glass includes work by John Blyth, Marcus McLundie and G. Maile Studios, Canterbury. The church hall (1897) is by William McClelland, major extensions to provide additional accommodation 1963 and 1983.

- Sunday: 11.00am
- Open last Wednesday of the month, May to September 2.00–4.00pm

81

ST COLUMBA'S PARISH CHURCH, AYR

Midton Road
Ayr
KA7 2SL

NS 337 208

Church of Scotland

www.ayrstcolumba.org.uk

Junction with Carrick Park.

Originally known as Trinity Church, Ayr, St Columba was dedicated in 1902. Built of red sandstone to designs by John B. Wilson of Glasgow. Fine pipe organ 1904 by J. J. Binns, restored by Harrison & Harrison 1985, Festival Trumpet added 2005. Stained glass by Sidney Holmes, C. C. Baillie, Susan Bradbury, Rowland Mitton and Moira Parker. Resurrection window unveiled by HRH the Princess Royal 2002. Cultured octagonal pencil tower with carillon of bells.

- Sunday: 9.30am and 11.15am, 1st Sunday of month 6.30pm
- Open 9.00am–12.00 noon, Monday, Tuesday, Thursday, Friday

82

ST JAMES'S PARISH CHURCH, AYR

Prestwick Road
Ayr
KA8 8LD

NS 342 232

Church of Scotland

Junction with Falkland Park Road.

St James's Church was built as a chapel of ease in 1885 to designs by John Murdoch. Murdoch, an engineer before he became an architect, was the most ambitious of the architects of Ayr in the late 19th century and received many important commissions. There is a rose window above the pulpit.

- Sunday: 11.00am
- Open by arrangement (01292 262420)

83 ST LEONARD'S, AYR

**St Leonard's Road
Ayr
KA7 2PR**

Ⱥ NS 338 204

🏠 Church of Scotland

Junction with Monument Road.

Built in 1886, several hundred metres from the site of the ancient chapel of St Leonard, the patron saint of prisoners. The architect was John Murdoch and the style belongs to the Geometric period of Decorated Gothic. The building comprises a nave with aisles, transepts and chancel (added 1911). Two-manual pipe organ by Harrison & Harrison, rebuilt 1992. Many beautiful stained glass windows.

- Sunday: 10.00am
- Open by arrangement (01292 263694)

84 ST PAUL'S CHURCH, AYR

**Peggieshill Road
Ayr
KA7 3RF**

Ⱥ NS 348 200

🏠 Roman Catholic

Linked with St Clare's Drongan, St Francis Waterside

The dedication stone was laid in 1966 and the church was opened 1967. Wall hanging by members of the parish depicts St Paul's meeting on the road to Damascus. Altar, lectern and baptismal font in Creetown granite.

- Sunday: 10.00am and 12.00 noon; daily usually at 10.00am
- Open by arrangement (01292 260197)

SOUTH AYRSHIRE

85 ST QUIVOX, AUCHINCRUIVE

Auchincruive
Ayr
KA6 5HJ

⚔ NS 375 241

🏛 Church of Scotland

B7035 off B743.

Christian presence on the site dates back to the 13th century. The medieval building was restored 1595 and extended 1767 to create a T-plan church. Interior fittings date largely from the late 18th century, including a good pulpit. In the kirkyard, mausoleum of the Campbells of Craigie, by W. H. Playfair 1822.

- Sunday: 11.30am
- Open by arrangement (01292 269746)

86 BALLANTRAE PARISH CHURCH

Main Street
Ballantrae
KA26 0NA

⚔ NX 084 825

🏛 Church of Scotland

🌐 www.ballantraeparishchurch.
org.uk

Linked with Glenapp

A77, 21km (13 miles) from Girvan.

Plain country kirk of 1819 given a Gothic flourish by a spiky bellcote (1891). Fine interior including a handsome Regency pulpit with a sweeping curved stair. Memorial to Lord Ballantrae. Nephew of Robert Burns was minister 1826–30. Kennedy aisle beside church. Ruins of Ardstinchar Castle close by.

- Sunday: 11.30am
- Open June to September 10.00am–
7.30pm daily (weather permitting)

87 BARR PARISH CHURCH

**Main Street
Barr
KA26 9TW**

NX 275 941

Church of Scotland

By Girvan on B734.

Dating from 1878, built to a design by A. Stevenson. Early Gothic gabled chapel. Slate roof, skew gables, rubble walls, freestone dressings. Picturesque south-east bellcote. Fine wooden ceiling. Restored 1978 P. J. Lorimer, London.

- Sunday: 12.00 noon
- Open all year 9.00am–7.00pm

 (July and August, Mon, Fri and Sat, 2.30–5.00pm)

88 COLMONELL CHURCH

**Colmonell
KA26 0SA**

NX 145 858

Church of Scotland

On A765.

Built in 1772, recast 1849 and renovated in 1899 by Robert Lorimer. Organ screen and chancel by Lorimer. Exceptional stained glass, including windows by Louis Davis and Douglas Strachan. Organ, 1899. Martyr's stone in graveyard from the time of the Covenanters, and Kennedy vault dating from 1620. Local lore gives a Christian presence here from AD c.600 when St Colman of Ella built his cell.

- Sunday: 10.00am
- List of keyholders in side porch

89 CRAIGIE PARISH CHURCH

Craigie
KA1 5LY

NS 427 323
Church of Scotland

Linked with Symington

4.8km (3 miles) south of Kilmarnock, off A77.

Pleasant traditional country kirk built 1776. T-plan with a bellcote, described in 1846 as 'a neat, plain edifice'. Close by are the remains of the previous church c.1580, but the site has been occupied by a church from medieval times.

- Sunday: 12.00 noon 1st and 3rd Sundays of the month
- Open by arrangement (01563 860384)

90 CROSSHILL PARISH CHURCH

Milton Street
Crosshill
KA19 7RG

NS 327 067
Church of Scotland

Linked with Dalrymple

On B7023.

White-harled T-plan traditional kirk of 1838, built as a chapel of ease to accommodate the population of what was then a new village based on domestic weaving. The interior was altered in the 1970s to form the present multipurpose building with church, hall, session house, kitchen and facilities within an unchanged exterior.

- Sunday: 12.00 noon
- Open by arrangement (01655 740241)

91 DUNDONALD PARISH CHURCH

**Main Street
Dundonald
KA2 9HG**

A NS 366 343

🏛 Church of Scotland

Tranquil setting for this traditional stone church of 1804, built on the site of an earlier building. The clock tower was added 1841, and the chancel 1906. Some fine stained glass, particularly Henry Dearle's unique *Last Supper*. Pipe organ, Norman & Beard 1906. Interesting grave stones in the tidy graveyard.

- Sunday: 11.00am
- Open by arrangement (01563 850243 or 01563 850703)

92 ST JOHN THE EVANGELIST, GIRVAN

**Piedmont Road
Girvan
KA26 0DS**

A NX 186 972

🏛 Scottish Episcopal

🌐 www.episcopalsouthayrshire.org.uk

Linked with Holy Trinity Ayr, St Oswald's Maybole

A simple rectangular nave church, designed by A. G. Thomson 1859. Chancel and the base of a tower added 1900, as first part of scheme for tower and transepts (see drawing in church). 16th-century screen, lectern, altar rails and other carvings, including bishop's throne from Holyrood in Edinburgh. Italian reredos. Painted shields represent various local county families.

- Sunday: Eucharist 9.45am
- Open by arrangement (01292 261145)

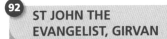

SOUTH AYRSHIRE

SACRED HEARTS OF JESUS & MARY, GIRVAN

**17 Harbour Street
Girvan
KA26 9AJ**

Ⱥ NX 183 979

⌂ Roman Catholic

A plain Gothic structure of 1860 with a huge prow-like porch added in 1959 by Stevenson & Ferguson. Stained glass windows of 1860.

- Saturday: 7.00pm; Sunday: 11.00am
- Open during daylight hours

GIRVAN METHODIST CHURCH

**Wesley Road
Girvan
KA26 9DD**

Ⱥ NX 185 977

⌂ Methodist

Junction with Dalrymple Street.

Red sandstone Arts & Crafts-style church with green slate steeply pitched and swept roof. Built in 1902 to replace Methodist chapel in Ailsa Street West. Two stained glass east windows and decorated wooden panels below a braced timber roof. Girvan was visited twice by John Wesley en route to Glasgow and Portpatrick, resulting in local Methodist worship.

- Sunday: 11.00am
- Open by arrangement (01465 713234)

95 GLENAPP CHURCH

**The Glen Kirk
Glenapp
KA26 0NY**

⚐ NX 075 746

⛪ Church of Scotland

🌐 www.ballantraeparishchurch.
org.uk

Linked with Ballantrae

On A77, 11.3km (7 miles) south of
Ballantrae.

Simple structure of 1850, enhanced
by Peter MacGregor Chalmers in 1910.
Windows by Douglas Strachan and
Kelley & Co. including a memorial
window to Elsie Mackay, 3rd daughter
of Earl of Inchcape, killed in 1928
attempting to fly the Atlantic. Modern
stained glass window above door, *The
Stilling of the Tempest*, in memory of 1st
Earl. Graveyard contains tombs of the
three Earls of Inchcape.

- Occasional services, details on
  website
- Open by arrangement (01465 831252
  or 01465 831393)

96 KIRKMICHAEL PARISH CHURCH

**80 Patna Road
Kirkmichael
KA19 7PJ**

⚐ NS 345 090

⛪ Church of Scotland

Linked with Straiton

3.2km (2 miles) east of Maybole.

Believed to stand on the site of a
13th-century church under the care of
the monks of Whithorn, the present
church was built 1787 by Hugh
Cairncross, and the belfry rebuilt
1887. Stone pulpit of 1919 depicting
St Michael, St George, St Andrew
and St Patrick incorporates the war
memorial. Two large stained glass
windows either side of the pulpit, one
by Christopher Whitworth Whall. The
oldest building is the lychgate; the
bell inside is dated 1702 and is still
rung when a bride leaves the church
after her wedding. Interesting stones
in surrounding graveyard, including
Covenanter's memorial, open every
day.

- Sunday: 10.30am
- Open by arrangement (01655 750286)

97 KIRKOSWALD PARISH CHURCH

Kirkoswald KA19 8HZ

NS 240 074

Church of Scotland

www.kirkoswald.net

Off A77, 8km (5 miles) south of Maybole and 11.3km (7 miles) north of Girvan.

Robert Adam 1777, contemporary with Culzean Castle. It is suggested that while working with Lord Cassillis, his client at Culzean, Robert Adam came across the church during construction and recommended some changes, giving the building fine Palladian details. The church was visited by Robert Burns and more recently by President Eisenhower. Following a fire, the church was fully restored in 1997 and the opportunity was taken to research the original Adam colour scheme. Burns's characters, Tam o' Shanter, Souter Johnnie and Kirkton Jean, are buried in the old graveyard, where also can be seen the baptismal font used to baptise Robert the Bruce.

- Sunday: 11.00am
- Open by arrangement (01655 760210 or 01655 760238)

98 ST OSWALD'S, MAYBOLE

Cargill Road Maybole KA19 8AF

NS 299 101

Scottish Episcopal

www.episcopalsouthayrshire.org.uk

Linked with Holy Trinity Ayr, St John's Girvan

Junction with Garden Path.

Pretty little building in 'English style' with apse and plain but tranquil interior. Built 1883 on land gifted to the church and seating about 90 people. Organ by Alfred Kirkland 1892. Hall and toilets added 1970s. Convenient for Maybole railway station.

- Sunday: 11.30am; Wednesday: 10.00am
- Open by arrangement (01655 882452)

99 OUR LADY & ST CUTHBERT, MAYBOLE

Dailly Road
Maybole
KA19 7AU

NS 299 094

Roman Catholic

www.olasc.org.uk

Gothic church with presbytery to west and hall to east, linked to form a T-plan complex. Built of yellow sandstone with white ashlar dressings with an octagonal spire on the north-west corner and a gabled porch at the north-east corner. Opened in 1878, the church has unusual bosses depicting the saints looking out into the church.

• Saturday: 6.30pm; Sunday: 10.00am
• Open by arrangement (01655 882145)

100 MONKTON COMMUNITY CHURCH

Main Street
Monkton
KA9 2RN

NS 357 277

Church of Scotland

www.mpnchurch.org.uk

Meeting place central to the local community, completed 2004 and designed by Fleming Muir Architects incorporating the old church hall. Three stained glass windows by Moira Parker on subjects representing the local and worldwide communities and including references to William Wallace, farming and fishing.

• 2nd and 4th Sundays of the month: 6.30pm
• Open by arrangement (01292 678810)

(Monday to Friday 11.00am–3.00pm)

SOUTH AYRSHIRE

101 MONKTON & PRESTWICK NORTH CHURCH

**10 Monkton Road
Prestwick
KA9 1AR**

A NS 353 263

Church of Scotland

⊕ www.mpnchurch.org.uk

The church was built as a Free Church in 1874, architect James Salmon & Son, and the bell-tower was added 1890, architect John Keppie. The congregation, united with the Church of Scotland in 1900, now uses a computerised communication system for hymn singing and visual aids. The pulpit, from St Cuthbert's, Monkton, is mobile. The original St Cuthbert's Communion Table has been fixed as a panel between two stained glass windows.

- Sunday: 11.00am
- Open by arrangement (01292 477499)

102 PRESTWICK SOUTH PARISH CHURCH

**Main Street
Prestwick
KA9 1NX**

A NS 352 260

Church of Scotland

⊕ www.south-church.org.uk

First church commission 1879 for James A. Morris, contemporary of Charles Rennie Mackintosh. Adept, light handling of Gothic forms, enlivened by Glasgow-style carving. Elegant spire with corner finials. Carefully chosen interior fittings include glass by Oscar Paterson.

- Sunday: 11.00am
- Open by arrangement (01292 478788)

103 KINGCASE PARISH CHURCH

**11 Waterloo Road
Prestwick
KA9 1AA**

⚔ NS 348 244

⛪ Church of Scotland

🌐 www.kingcase.freeserve.co.uk

Behind Aldi store.

Red sandstone cruciform church. Built in 1912, the transepts were added in 1956. Four beautiful stained glass windows, three of the 1950s and one of a contemporary design. The south wall has a cross with a lamb motif in it.

• Sunday: 9.45am and 11.15am
• Open by arrangement with Church Office (01292 470755) Monday to Friday 9.30am–12.30pm

104 ST QUIVOX, PRESTWICK

**St Quivox Road
Prestwick
KA9 1LU**

⚔ NS 352 257

⛪ Roman Catholic

The building was completed in 1933 and is built of Accrington brick in Romanesque style. Extended in 1969, incorporating the old building to form a rectangular-shaped church. Inside are a sanctuary mosaic panel and the Stations of the Cross. Jubilee 2000 window.

• Sunday: 10.00am, 11.30am and 6.00pm
• Open daily 10.00am–5.00pm

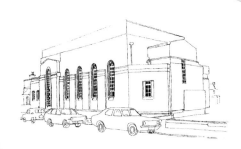

SOUTH AYRSHIRE

105 STRAITON PARISH CHURCH

**St Cuthbert's
Straiton
KA19 7NE**

⚔ NS 380 049

⛪ Church of Scotland

Linked with Kirkmichael

6.4km (4 miles) east of Kirkmichael.

The main part of the church dates from 1758. The piscina of the original church is still visible on the east wall. Chantry chapel of late 15th century containing various memorial plaques to members of the Hunter Blair family. In 1901 the church was renovated by John Kinross and the bell-tower was added to the design of John Murdoch. Beautiful carvings on the ceiling and pulpit. Striking *Millennium Banner* mounted on a pedestal made from a former pew. Tapestry cushions, 1993, depict themes from the life and work of the community, and artwork by the local Sewing Guild commemorates 1997 as 'The Year of Faith'; 1998 as 'The Year of Hope'; and 1999 as 'The Year of Love'. The stone font is the gift of the Fergusson family. Splendid stained glass. Covenanter's memorial in graveyard, open every day.

- Sunday: 12.00 noon
- Open by arrangement (01655 750286)

106 SYMINGTON CHURCH

**Symington
KA1 5QP**

⚔ NS 384 314

⛪ Church of Scotland

🌐 www.symingtonchurch.com

Linked with Craigie

Off A77, 3,2km (2 miles) from Prestwick Airport,

Known as Ayrshire's Norman church, the rectangular building with 1m (3ft) thick walls was founded c.1160 by Symon de Loccard whose own story in itself makes a visit worthwhile. Restored 1919 by Peter MacGregor Chalmers. Norman arched windows, piscina and ancient oak-beamed ceiling. The stained glass, much of it by Douglas Strachan, is glorious in creation and colour. Though small in size, its stones breathe the atmosphere of prayer and praise of all the saints over 800 years.

- Sunday: 10.30am
- Open by arrangement (01563 830289 or 01563 830043)

TROON OLD CHURCH

**Ayr Street
Troon
KA10 6EB**

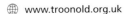 NS 321 309

Church of Scotland

www.troonold.org.uk

Neo-Gothic building in red sandstone by Hippolyte Blanc and dedicated in 1895. The stained glass of the Ascension window is by the Morris Studio; other windows by Gordon Webster. Alabaster reredos depicting Moses, St Paul and the Last Supper has a finely carved canopy and stands above a mosaic pavement of the Paschal Lamb. Richly carved pulpit, communion table and font. Various memorials.

- Sunday: 10.30am; Wednesday: 11.15am
- Open Tuesday, Thursday, Friday and Saturday 10.00am–12.00 noon

 (by arrangement)

(Saturday and Sunday)

---

108 OUR LADY & ST MEDDAN, TROON

**4 Cessnock Road
Troon
KA10 6NJ**

NS 327 311

Roman Catholic

Built in 1910, the design for this church by Reginald Fairlie takes inspiration from a number of sources including the Church of the Holy Rude in Stirling. Nave with buttresses between the windows and a powerful tower at the west end with attached stair tower topped with a delightful crown spire with finials. Major restoration in 1990s.

- Saturday Vigil Mass: 6.00pm; Sunday Mass: 9.00am and 11.15am
- Open daily until 4.00pm

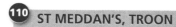

109 PORTLAND PARISH CHURCH, TROON

**South Beach
Troon
KA10 6NN**

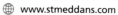

⚔ NS 323 308

🏛 Church of Scotland

🌐 www.troonportlandchurch.org.uk

Junction with St Meddan's Street.

Opened in 1914 as a United Free Church by H. E. Clifford & Lunan. Perpendicular Gothic in white sandstone with fine tracery in the great north window which is repeated in the nave windows. Interior has exposed stone with blonde Austrian oak pews and fittings. The stained glass chancel window was donated in 1920 as a war memorial by Mr A. F. Steven. Harrison & Harrison two-manual organ, rebuilt 1970. Halls extension added 1964.

- Sunday: 10.30am
- Open July and August, Sunday and Thursday 2.00–4.30pm

110 ST MEDDAN'S, TROON

**Church Street
Troon
KA10 6HT**

⚔ NS 323 309

🏛 Church of Scotland

🌐 www.stmeddans.com

Junction with St Meddan's Street.

Built 1888–9 for the United Presbyterian Church, architect J. B. Wilson, St Meddan's has many noteworthy features. The tall and stately spire houses a clock which was originally part of the University of Glasgow's Old College in High Street, Glasgow. Many beautiful stained glass windows; the largest, opposite the pulpit, depicts the healing of Jairus's daughter. The image of the windows made fourth place in 'Treasured Places' in 2008.

- Sunday: 10.30am
- Open Monday, Tuesday and Thursday 9.00am–2.00pm

111 ST NINIAN'S, TROON

**Bentinck Drive
Troon
KA10 6HX**

⚔ NS 327 304

🏛 Scottish Episcopal

Designed in Arts & Crafts Gothic by James A. Morris, nave dedicated 1913, chancel built and dedicated 1921. Twenty years of planning culminated when the church was consecrated in 1931. The church contains many examples of fine woodwork by Yorkshire carver Robert Thomson of Kilburn, whose signature is the carved mouse (look closely at the main door). Organ by J. J. Binns, rebuilt 1987.

- Sunday: 8.00am Holy Communion, 10.30am; Sung Eucharist 1st and 3rd Sunday; Wednesday: 10.00am Holy Communion
- Open daily 9.30am–4.00pm

112 ARDWELL CHURCH

**Ardwell
DG9 9LX**

⚔ NX 100 457

🏛 Church of Scotland

🌐 www.ardwell-church.org.uk

Linked with Kirkmaiden, St Medan's Drummore, Sandhead

0.8km (½ mile) west of Ardwell village.

Surrounded by trees and shrubs and fronted with grass and flowerbeds, Gothic cruciform church by Peter MacGregor Chalmers 1901. Tower with octagonal spire and corner pinnacles. Notable inside are the inscriptions in the masonry. Pulpit, reredos, screen and communion table in oak, elaborately carved. Stained glass window of *The Calming of the Storm*.

- Sunday: every two weeks (normally) 10.00am
- Open by arrangement (01776 830215)

113 ALL SAINTS' CHURCH, CHALLOCH

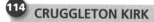

**Challoch
DG8 6RB**

NX 385 675

Scottish Episcopal

3.2km (2 miles) north of Newton Stewart on A714.

Built as private chapel of Edward James Stopford-Blair of Penninghame House and consecrated 1872. Designed by W. G. Habershon & Pite of London and an excellent example of a small Victorian church. Ten stained glass windows, 17 memorial plaques, pine altar and wrought-iron and brass rood screen. Fine Harston two-tracker organ 1881, restored 1993.

- Sunday: 9.00am Holy Eucharist, 10.30am Matins (1st Sunday), Sung Eucharist (2nd, 4th and 5th), Family Communion (3rd). Saints days as advertised.
- Open by arrangement (01671 402101)

114 CRUGGLETON KIRK

**Cruggleton Farm
Cruggleton
DG8 8HL**

NX 478 428

Non-denominational

Linked with Kirkinner, Sorbie

4.8km (3 miles) south of Garlieston on B7063.

The most complete Romanesque church in the area. Former chapel of Cruggleton Castle set in a walled burial ground, restored 1890s by William B. M. Galloway for the 3rd Marquess of Bute. The outside is largely a conjectural reconstruction with new work delineated by a line of red tiles. Inside, the magnificent chancel arch is mostly of the 12th century.

- Ecumenical service, involving Church of Scotland, Roman Catholic and Episcopal communities, on 1st Sunday of September each year, 3.00pm
- Open by arrangement (01988 600237)

115 ST MEDAN'S, DRUMMORE

**Stair Street
Drummore
DG9 9PT**

 NX 135 367

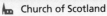 Church of Scotland

Linked with Ardwell, Kirkmaiden, Sandhead

Built 1903 in red Dumfries sandstone with an attractive roof of red and yellow pine. Hymnus IV electronic organ. Morrison memorial window behind choir 1951. John McGuffog memorial window above pulpit, designed and made by Arthur C. Speirs DA of Greenock 1996.

- Sunday: 11.30am
- Open by arrangement (01776 840210)

116 GLASSERTON CHURCH

**Glasserton
DG8 8NB**

 NX 422 381

 Church of Scotland

Linked with St Ninian's Whithorn, Isle of Whithorn

0.4km (¼ mile) south-west of junction of A746 and A747.

Former estate church of 1722 with north aisle and tower added 1836, designed by J. B. Papworth. Simple stone rectangle with round-headed windows. Roofless mausoleum attached to the church contains the 16th-century memorial of Lady Grizel Gordon, Lady Garleis. Good 18th-century headstones.

- First and last Sunday of month: 11.30am
- Open by arrangement (01988 500459)

DUMFRIES & GALLOWAY

WIGTOWNSHIRE

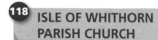

117 OLD LUCE CHURCH, GLEN LUCE

**Church Street
Glenluce
DG8 0QA**

𝒜 NX 200 576

⛪ Church of Scotland

Linked with New Luce

On A75.

T-plan kirk on top of the hill. Built 1814 and renovated and given a chancel in 1968 by Hill, Macdonald & Potter. Two stained glass windows in the vestibule by William Meikle, 1905, and a large round stained glass window in the chancel. The organ by Casey & Cairney, 1968, is beautiful in tone and appearance. Pulpit, communion table and font in oak and white Sicilian marble. Every Sunday is a celebration!

- Sunday: 11.45am
- Open by arrangement (01581 300319)

118 ISLE OF WHITHORN PARISH CHURCH

**Main Street
Isle of Whithorn
DG8 8LG**

𝒜 NX 478 363

⛪ Church of Scotland

Linked with St Ninian's Whithorn, Glasserton

Former Free Church of 1844 on a spectacular location on the foreshore of this picturesque village with its natural harbour. Simple white rectangle with bellcote. Heritage display telling the story of the church today and village life in the past.

- Middle Sunday of month: 11.30am
- Open daily April to October

119 KIRKCOWAN PARISH CHURCH

**Main Street
Kirkcowan
DG8 0HP**

⚔ NX 327 610

⛪ Church of Scotland

Linked with Wigtown

At the west end of the village, built in 1834 to replace a former church, of which only an ivy-clad east gable remains in its kirkyard (east end of village). The present church is a harled T-plan building with external stairs at the east and west gables leading to two galleries. A tower at the north side. Inside, three galleries in all, supported by marbled cast-iron columns. Tall pulpit of 1834 and a late 19th-century chamber organ by J. & A. Mirrlees, brought here in 1966.

- Sunday: 11.30am
- Open by arrangement (01671 830645)

120 KIRKINNER PARISH CHURCH

**Main Street
Kirkinner
DG8 9AL**

⚔ NX 423 515

⛪ Church of Scotland

Linked with Sorbie, Cruggleton

A simple rural parish church with tower, built 1828. Galleried interior. Contains the magnificent carved stone Kirkinner Cross created at Whithorn in the 12th century.

- Sunday: 10.45am
- Open by arrangement (01988 840643)

DUMFRIES & GALLOWAY

WIGTOWNSHIRE

 121 **KIRKMAIDEN OLD KIRK**

**Kirkmaiden
DG9 9QS**

Ⓐ NX 139 324

🏠 Church of Scotland

Linked with Ardwell, St Medan's
Drummore, Sandhead

Mull of Galloway.

Built 1638 to replace St Catherine's
at Mull of Galloway in the most
southerly parish in Scotland.
T-shaped church with vaults of the
McDouall family of Logan underneath
balcony. 'Treacle' Bible on display.
Bell from Clanyard Castle, a gift
from the Earl of Dalhousie 1532.
The graveyard has fine 18th-century
gravestones including one in the
form of a lighthouse.

- Sunday: 11.30am last Sunday May to
  September
- Open daily March to October,
  10.00am–5.00pm, or by arrangement
  (01776 840601)

 122 **MOCHRUM CHURCH**

**Main Street
Mochrum
DG8 9LU**

Ⓐ NX 347 463

🏠 Church of Scotland

3.2km (2 miles) north of Port William.

Traditional T-plan kirk built in 1794
on the site of a previous church.
Birdcage bellcote. The building has
no internal stairs but has six doors
and forestairs for the galleries on
three sides inside. Organ by Walker,
moved here from Penpont in 1973.

- Sunday: 11.00am
- Open by arrangement (01988 700534)

123 NEW LUCE CHURCH

New Luce
DG8 0AJ

🏛 NX 175 645

⛪ Church of Scotland

Linked with Old Luce

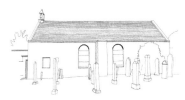

South end of New Luce, 9.7km
(6 miles) north of Glenluce.

New Luce church was founded in 1647
when the original Parish of Glenluce
was divided into Old Luce and
New Luce. The famous Covenanter
Alexander Peden preached as
minister, 1660–3. The present church,
dating from 1821, is of rectangular
plan with a birdcage bellcote over the
west gable. Vestry added 1957.

- Sunday: 10.00am
- Open by arrangement: Mr James
  Kilpatrick, Craigdhu, Main Street,
  New Luce

124 PENNINGHAME ST JOHN'S CHURCH, NEWTON STEWART

Church Street
Newton Stewart
DG8 6HG

🏛 NX 410 654

⛪ Church of Scotland

🌐 www.penninghameparish.org.uk

Church Street is parallel to town's
main street.

Church completed in 1840 to a design
by William Burn. Groome's *Gazetteer*
describes it as 'a handsome Gothic
edifice'. Organ by J. F. Harston of
Newark in 1878, believed to be the
largest and most intact of all organs
built by him; renovated by Hill,
Norman & Beard 1962. Spire 46m
(151ft). Tower clock with 10m (32ft)
pendulum, 1880, by James Ritchie of
Edinburgh, restored 2004. All glass
replaced 1996. Interesting display of
Communion silver including two
chalices dated 1711.

- Sunday: 10.30am
- Open by arrangement (01671 402543)

DUMFRIES & GALLOWAY

WIGTOWNSHIRE

125 OUR LADY & ST NINIAN, NEWTON STEWART

Windsor Road
Newton Stewart
DG8 6HP

Å NX 409 658

⌂ Roman Catholic

⊕ www.rcmachars.org.uk

Linked with St Martin's Whithorn, Sacred Heart Wigtown

Simple Gothic church built of grey stone with red sandstone margins to the windows, 1875–6 by Goldie & Child of London. Nave and chancel under a continuous slate roof, the skyline given interest by the tall gabled belfry over the picturesque red-painted wooden porch.

- Sunday: 10.00am; Monday: 10.00am
- Open by arrangement (01671 402182)

126 SANDHEAD CHURCH

Main Street
Sandhead
DG9 9JF

Å NX 097 500

⌂ Church of Scotland

⊕ www.ardwell-church.org.uk

Linked with Ardwell, Kirkmaiden, St Medan's Drummore

Substantial timber construction with steeply pitched tiled roof and cedarboard-clad walls by architects Goudie & Hill 1962. The unusual structure uses laminated timber portal frames with obscured glass between the frames in both side walls. Flat-roofed porch with masonry bell-tower. Internally, much varnished wood. Inverted-pyramid-shaped pulpit.

- Sunday: every two weeks, normally 10.00am
- Open by arrangement (01776 830215)

 (2.00–4.00pm, Wednesday and Sunday in summer)

127 SORBIE PARISH CHURCH

Millisle
Garlieston
DG8 8AF

 NX 468 464
Church of Scotland

Linked with Kirkinner, Cruggleton

Church with tower and spire built of whinstone with red sandstone dressings, 1873–6, designed by David Thomson. Stunning stained glass: St Martin by Christopher Whall, south transept window of St Paul by Morris & Co. to a design by Burne-Jones, east window of the Ascension. The organ came from the Cally Palace and is of unusual design.

• Sunday: 10.00am
• Open by arrangement (01988 600610)

128 SOUTHWICK PARISH CHURCH

Caulkerbush
DG2 8AJ

NX 927 574
Church of Scotland

Linked with Colvend, Kirkbean

On B793, near junction with A710.

Standing by woodland just outside the policies of Southwick House, a stone church of local grey granite with dressings of red sandstone. By Peddie & Kinnear 1891, a mixture of Early Christian and Norman. Its crossing tower was derived from the 14th-century tower of St Monans Parish Church. Neo-Norman font by Cox & Buckley 1898 and a Neo-Jacobean pulpit. Wrought-iron Arts & Crafts light fittings, once for oil lamps. Late 19th-century stained glass. Organ replaced in May 1999 with Ahlborn SL100.

• Sunday: 10.00am
• Open by arrangement (01387 880662)

DUMFRIES & GALLOWAY

WIGTOWNSHIRE

129 ST NINIAN'S PRIORY CHURCH, WHITHORN

**Bruce Street
Whithorn
DG8 8PY**

⋏ NX 444 403

⛪ Church of Scotland

Linked with Isle of Whithorn, Glasserton

Built 1822 with later 19th-century tower. Simple rectangular hall church. Carved oak pulpit. Stained glass east windows gifted by the daughter of Gemmell Hutcheson RSA in memory of her father. Located on the site of Whithorn 'dig' in the former precincts of Whithorn Priory. First Scottish Christian community founded here by St Ninian, pre-dates Iona.

- Sunday: 10.00am and 7.00pm
- Open Easter to end of October, 10.00am–5.00pm

130 ST MARTIN & ST NINIAN, WHITHORN

**George Street
Whithorn
DG8 8PZ**

⋏ NX 446 401

⛪ Roman Catholic

🌐 www.rcmachars.org.uk

Linked with Our Lady Newton Stewart, Sacred Heart Wigtown

Cruciform church of nave, chancel and transepts by Goodhart-Rendel, Broadbent & Curtis, 1959–60. The grey harl and slate roofs are given character by the wide entrance gable topped with a double belfry above a pointed arched window surmounting the square porch.

- Sunday: 12.00 noon; Friday: 10.00am
- Open by arrangement (01671 402182)

131 WIGTOWN PARISH CHURCH

**Bank Street
Wigtown
DG8 9HT**

Å NX 436 555

🏠 Church of Scotland

Linked with Kirkcowan

The parish church on an ancient ecclesiastical site, largely rebuilt in 1730, was by the middle of the next century thought to be 'an old mean-looking edifice'. A new church, by the London architect Henry Roberts, was built nearby in 1851, still using the Georgian T-plan with a French pavilion roof on the tower. Built of granite, it encloses a broad nave and east transept. Peter MacGregor Chalmers added a communion table and font, an organ chamber, and rearranged the seating in 1914. In the transept are three carved stones, one a Celtic cross shaft decorated on both faces with interlaced rings, similar to those of the same period at Whithorn. Stained glass in the east transept window by James Ballantine & Son 1867.

- Sunday: 10.00am
- Open Easter to September, Monday to Friday 2.00–4.00pm

132 SACRED HEART, WIGTOWN

**South Main Street
Wigtown
DG8 9EH**

Å NX 434 553

🏠 Roman Catholic

🌐 www.rcmachars.org.uk

Linked with Our Lady Newton Stewart, St Martin Whithorn

Simple brick-built Gothic church of nave and apse by J. Garden Brown, 1879. The door sits within a shallow gabled porch, the line echoing the line of the gable. Four lancet windows support a niche containing a statue of Jesus Christ.

- Sunday: 6.00pm; Tuesday: 10.00am
- Open by arrangement (01671 402182)

133 BALMACLELLAN CHURCH

**Balmaclellan
DG7 3QE**

🅰 NX 651 791
🏛 Church of Scotland

Linked with Carsphairn, Dalry, Kells

On A712, 3.2km (2 miles) east of New Galloway.

A harled, T-plan kirk, the body was built in 1753, with the north aisle added in 1833 by William McCandlish. The stained glass west window is dated 1928 and is by Gordon Webster. The graveyard has an early 18th-century table-stone commemorating the Covenanting martyr Robert Grierson. Statue and plaque in churchyard commemorate Sir Walter Scott's 'Old Mortality', who came from Balmaclellan.

- First Sunday of every month: 12.00 noon
- Open by arrangement (01644 430380)

134 CARSPHAIRN PARISH CHURCH

**Carsphairn
DH7 3TQ**

🅰 NX 563 932
🏛 Church of Scotland

Linked with Dalry, Kells, Balmaclellan

On A713, 16.1km (10 miles) north of St John's Town of Dalry.

Rectangular hall-church of 1815 built to replace church of 1636 destroyed by fire. Apse added and interior reordered late 19th or early 20th century. Central communion table. Memorials including John Semple, Covenanting minister, and John Loudon MacAdam, roads pioneer. Covenanter's grave.

- Sunday: 10.30am
- Carsphairn Pastoral and Horticultural Show, first Saturday in June
- Open by arrangement (01644 460208)

135 COLVEND PARISH CHURCH

Colvend
DG5 4QN

NX 862 541

Church of Scotland

Linked with Kirkbean, Southwick

0.8km (½ mile) from A710 on road to Rockliffe.

A chaste Early Christian church by Peter MacGregor Chalmers 1911, of granite with red sandstone dressings and set on a rise overlooking the Solway Firth. Its bell-tower is topped by a steep pyramid roof. A pretty interior with nave, aisle and transept and a timbered roof. Plain plastered walls are a foil for the sandstone columns which support round-headed arches springing from cushion capitals to form arcades into the aisle and transept. In the chancel, the deep colour of the stained glass window, the *Ascension* by Stephen Adam & Co. 1918, forms a lovely backdrop to the High Presbyterian arrangement of furnishings. Other windows by Adam & Co. and by Margaret Chilton and Marjorie Kemp 1926.

- Sunday: 11.30am
- Open daily 10.00am–6.00pm

136 CORSOCK CHURCH

Corsock
DG7 3DL

NX 762 760

Church of Scotland

www.ckpc.org.uk

Linked with Crossmichael, Parton, Kirkpatrick Durham

On A712.

Built as a Free Church, 1851–2 by William McCandlish, chancel and chancel arch added 1912 by J. A. McGregor from a design by James Kennedy Hunter. Several stained glass windows, some from the old parish church. Memorial plaque and stained glass window commemorate James Clerk Maxwell.

- Sunday: 11.00am
- Open by arrangement (01644 440279)

137 CROSSMICHAEL CHURCH

**Crossmichael
DG7 3AU**

⚔ NX 729 670

🏠 Church of Scotland

Linked with Parton, Kirkpatrick Durham, Corsock

North end of village on A713.

T-plan church with tall pointed windows, 1751. The unusual round tower is probably 1611 – the date of the bell by Burgerhuys. North aisle added by David McLellan 1822, vestry 1963 and porch 1971. Remarkably complete early 19th-century interior. Stained glass by Heaton, Butler & Bayne, 1898. Notable monuments in graveyard: headstone of Covenanter William Graham, burial enclosure of the Gordons of Culvennan and classical monument of William Gordon of Greenlaw.

- Sunday: 9.30am or 11.00am except 1st Sunday of the month
- Open by arrangement (01556 503645)

138 ST PETER'S CHURCH, DALBEATTIE

**Craignair Street
Dalbeattie
DG5 4AX**

⚔ NX 831 613

🏠 Roman Catholic

The oldest post-Reformation Roman Catholic church in Galloway. Hall church 1814 of pinky granite with red sandstone dressings. Grey granite tower added c.1850. Priest's house attached.

- Sunday Mass: 9.00am and 11.00am
- Open daily 9.00am–5.00pm

139 ST MARY'S, GATEHOUSE OF FLEET

**Dromore Road
Gatehouse of Fleet
DG7 2BP**

NX 597 562

Scottish Episcopal

www.greyfriarsstmarys.org.uk

Linked with Greyfriars Kirkcudbright

Episcopalians in the area worshipped in the private chapel of Cally House until the present building of 1840 was purchased from the United Presbyterian Church and dedicated to St Mary in 1909. It is probably unique among Scottish Episcopal Churches in having a stained glass window commemorating John Knox!

- Sunday: 9.30am Eucharist; Wednesday: 9.45am Holy Communion
- Open by arrangement (01557 330146)

140 KIRKBEAN PARISH CHURCH

**Kirkbean
DG2 8DW**

NX 980 592

Church of Scotland

Linked with Colvend, Southwick

A710, 8km (5 miles) south of New Abbey.

Harled T-plan kirk said to have been designed by William Craik, sometime Laird of Arbigland. The tower on the west wall is of two lower stages, 1776, with a Diocletian window in its second stage, and two upper stages added in 1836 are by Walter Newall, the first with a clock, and the top with a big octagonal belfry cupola of polished ashlar under a lantern. Venetian window in the east gable of the tail of the church. Inside, plain furnishings of 1883. A memorial font, presented by the United States Navy in memory of John Paul Jones, a gardener's son from Arbigland, who founded it; designed and sculpted by George Henry Paulin 1946.

- Sunday: 10.00am
- Open by arrangement (01387 880662)

141 KIRKCUDBRIGHT PARISH CHURCH

**St Mary Street
Kirkcudbright
DG6 4EL**

⚔ NX 683 509

⛪ Church of Scotland

🌐 www.kirkcudbrightparish.org.uk

The present Neo-Gothic building dates from 1838 and was designed by William Burn. Cruciform in shape, the nave and gallery together comprise the 'Country End', with the south transept referred to as the 'Town End' and the north transept as the 'Trades End'. A substantial pulpit, also designed by Burn, incorporates a sounding board and a precentor's box. Stained glass window of 1913 in south transept by William Meikle in memory of the Rev. A. C. Campbell.

- Sunday: 9.30am all year, and 6.30pm on 2nd Sunday of the month
- Open June to August, 9.00am–5.00pm, or by arrangement (01557 331217)

142 GREYFRIARS, KIRKCUDBRIGHT

**Kirkcudbright
DG6 4HZ**

⚔ NS 682 511

⛪ Scottish Episcopal

🌐 www.greyfriarsstmarys.org.uk

Linked with St Mary's Gatehouse

The sanctuary of Greyfriars Church is the last remaining fragment of a Franciscan friary. Dating from either the 13th or 15th centuries, it has undergone many changes in both design and use over the years. The MacClellan Monument, erected in 1597, is one of the most interesting features of the church. On the left of the high altar is an ancient piscina. There are also three fine modern stained glass windows including work by Gordon Webster. The cross and candlesticks are the work of Mabel Brunton, a distinguished member of the artists' colony which flourished in the town in the 1920s. Other interesting furnishings are the 17th-century dower chest and the medieval holy water stoup.

- Sunday: 8.00am Holy Communion, 11.30am Eucharist; Thursday: 10.00am Holy Communion
- Open by arrangement (01557 330146)

143 KIRKPATRICK DURHAM CHURCH

**Kirkpatrick Durham
DG7 3HB**

⚔ NX 785 699
⛪ Church of Scotland
🌐 www.ckpd.org.uk

Linked with Crossmichael, Parton, Corsock

On road to Bridge of Urr.

Built 1849–50 by architect Walter Newall; the T-plan church with tower is late Georgian in design despite the Victorian date. Interior reordered 1949 and a partition constructed which allowed a hall to be created. Upper hall constructed 1968–9. Refurbishment 2002.

- Sunday: 9.30am or 11.00am except 1st Sunday of the month
- Open by arrangement (01556 650230)

144 MONIGAFF PARISH CHURCH

**Minnigaff
DG8 6SH**

⚔ NX 410 666
⛪ Church of Scotland

Near Newton Stewart.

Neo-Gothic church with tower completed in 1836 to a design by William Burn. Stained glass by William Wailes of Newcastle 1868 and Ballantine, Edinburgh 1910. Font from Earl of Galloway's private chapel. Organ built in 1873, Bryceson Brothers, London. Ruins of pre-Reformation church on medieval foundations. East gable 12th- or early 13th-century. Motte and ditch. Eighth-century stone slab of Irish missionary influence. Grave stones including B-listed Heron monument. Yew tree 900 years old. Historical display.

- Sunday: 10.00am; 1st Sunday of month Holy Communion 9.25am
- Open July and August, Monday and Friday 2.00–4.30pm, or by arrangement (01671 402164)

145 NEW ABBEY CHURCH

**Main Street
New Abbey
DG2 8BY**

🏛 NX 965 659

⛪ Church of Scotland

Built 1876–7 by James Barbour of Dumfries using stones from Kindar Mill. T-plan Gothic church of squared granite blocks with red sandstone dressings. Timber roof replaced after a fire in 1963. Low octagonal pulpit. Stained glass window, 1915, design by William Morris from a Burne-Jones drawing, in memory of Rev. Dr James Stewart Wilson, Minister 1863–1909.

- Sunday: 10.00am
- Open daily April to September, otherwise by arrangement (01387 850232)

146 KELLS PARISH CHURCH, NEW GALLOWAY

**Kirk Road
New Galloway
DG7 3RS**

🏛 NX 632 784

⛪ Church of Scotland

Linked with Carsphairn, Dalry, Balmaclellan

Built in 1822 to a design by William McCandlish. A granite T-plan church with three-stage square tower at the centre of south wall. Interior mainly reconstructed in 1911 following original layout. Galleries on three sides with pulpit on long south wall. Notable churchyard with three 'Adam and Eve' stones of 1706–7, and a delightful upright for Captain Gordon's gamekeeper, John Murray.

- Sunday: 10.30am, not 1st Sunday
- Open by arrangement (01644 430380)

147 ST MARGARET'S, NEW GALLOWAY

**New Galloway
DG7 3RP**

NX 636 778

Scottish Episcopal

On edge of New Galloway on Ken Bridge road.

Picturesque Arts & Crafts church of 1904 by W. M. Harrison, the chancel added 1908 and the lychgate 1912. The walls of the church are harled and the roofs are red-tiled. The wooden panelling and furnishings are a mixture of Oregon pine and oak and the windows are variously by Kempe, Clayton & Bell, and James Powell & Sons.

- Sunday and Wednesday: 10.30am
- Key at Rectory next door or by arrangement (01644 420235)

148 PARTON KIRK

**Kilennan
Parton
DG7 3NE**

NX 696 699

Church of Scotland

Linked with Crossmichael, Kirkpatrick Durham, Corsock

On A713.

A kirk, dedicated to St Inan or St Ninian and known as Kilennan, existed at Parton in 1296. The kirk was rebuilt in 1534 and its ruins stand in the churchyard. A new church with battlemented tower was built 1834, designed by Walter Newall. The interior was remodelled in the late 19th century. Burial place of William Macmath, who saved many old Border ballads, and of James Clerk Maxwell, eminent scientist.

- Sunday: 9.30am or 11.00am, except 1st Sunday of the month
- Open by arrangement (01644 470210) or key held at Smiddy House, Parton

149 ST JOHN'S TOWN OF DALRY

**Main Street
St John's Town of Dalry
DG7 3QE**

NX 618 813

Church of Scotland

Linked with Carsphairn, Kells, Balmaclellan

On A713.

Completed in 1831 to a design by William McCandlish to replace a ruinous building of 1771; probably the third church to occupy the site. Early records are scarce, but a dilapidated church, existed in 1427. Traditional T-shaped interior, plainly furnished. Pulpit with carved wooden canopy. Galleries on three sides. Stands near the Water of Ken with wide views of the Rhinns of Kells. Avenue of lime trees. Interesting old kirkyard with Covenanters' stone and Gordon Aisle, burial place of the Gordons of Lochinvar. Robert Burns fashioned his poem 'Tam o' Shanter' on a local tale.

- Sunday: 12.00 noon October to April, 9.00am May to September
- Open by arrangement (01644 430273)

150 TROQUEER PARISH CHURCH, DUMFRIES

**Troqueer Road
Dumfries
DG2 7DF**

NX 975 751

Church of Scotland

www.troqueerparishchurch.com

This red sandstone church, rebuilt in 1771 and altered in the Gothic style by James Barbour in 1887, has a simple rectangular shape, a horseshoe gallery, two entrance porches, a memorial vestry (1954) and a corbelled birdcage belfry. Interesting memorials, notably to Covenanting Minister John Blackadder and two posthumous VCs. Four stained glass memorial windows from the former Laurieknowe Church.

- Sunday: 11.00am and 6.30pm
- Open by arrangement (01387 253043)

151 ANNAN OLD PARISH CHURCH

Church Street
Annan
DG12 6DS

NY 196 666

Church of Scotland

Linked with Dornock

East end of High Street.

The original town church was near the town hall; the present church was built in 1791 and the imposing steeple, the first classical steeple in the area, was added in 1798. The cost was £602 4s. 3d. The galleried interior was altered 1870. One of the congregation's most famous sons was the theologian and millenarian Edward Irving (1792–1834) who was deposed by the Kirk Session and locked out!

- Sunday: 11.15am all year and 6.30pm September to Easter
- Open by arrangement (01461 201405)

152 ST ANDREW'S PARISH CHURCH, ANNAN

15 Bank Street
Annan
DG12 6AA

NY 194 665

Church of Scotland

Linked with Brydekirk

Originally St Andrew's United Free Presbyterian Church, built 1834–5, by William Gregan. Classical façade given dignity by pilasters supporting a pediment and central tower. Its interior of yellow pine gives a lightness to any act of worship. Some of the stained glass windows, the font and vestibule table are war memorials. The two-manual pipe organ was built in 1914.

- Sunday: 11.15am, and 6.00pm last Sunday of month (in the hall)
- Open by arrangement (01461 202626)

153 ST COLUMBA'S CHURCH, ANNAN

**Scott's Street
Annan
DG12 6JG**

Å NY 199 665

🏠 Roman Catholic

Linked with Holy Trinity Lockerbie, St Francis Langholm, St Luke's Moffat

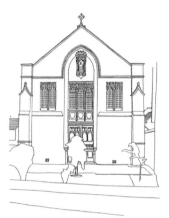

Built as a Congregational Church in 1794 on the site of a Secession Meeting House and reopened as a Catholic Church in 1839. Extended at both ends in 1904 by Charles Walker of Newcastle as the gift of the parish priest the Rev. Lord Archibald Douglas. Stations of the Cross by Brendan Ellis 1984. Painted panels by Joe Burns 1997.

- Saturday Vigil Mass: 6.00pm; Sunday Mass: 12.00 noon
- Key from adjacent presbytery (01461 202776)

154 ST JOHN THE EVANGELIST, ANNAN

**St John's Road
Annan
DG12 6AW**

Å NY 194 664

🏠 Scottish Episcopal

Linked with St John's Eastriggs, All Saints' Gretna, All Saints' Lockerbie, St John's Moffat

One of the oldest episcopal churches in the diocese, being built in 1843. Gothic church in red sandstone with nave, chancel and tall bellcote on the west gable, designed by Christopher Hodgson of Carlisle. East window depicting St John the Evangelist, by Mayer & Co, 1892. Chancel is lined with very fine oak panelling matching the carved altar, pulpit and eagle lectern. Church hall of 1893 in the grounds.

- Sunday: 9.30am (9.45am on 2nd Sunday of the month)
- Open by arrangement (01461 202869)

155 APPLEGARTH, SIBBALDIE & JOHNSTONE CHURCH

Applegarth
DG11 1SX

NY 104 843

Church of Scotland

Linked with Lochmaben

North end of village, 4.8km (3 miles) north-west of Lockerbie.

There has been a church here since 1140; the churches of Applegarth and Sibbaldie united in 1609, and with Johnstone in 2004. White T-plan kirk of 1763, remodelled 1885. Two rose windows and two other windows with stained glass, erected as a war memorial in 1920. Attached is the exceptional burial enclosure of the Jardines, late 17th-century with classical detailing.

- Sunday: 10.15am
- Open by arrangement (01387 811319)

156 BRYDEKIRK PARISH CHURCH

Bridge Street
Brydekirk
DG12 5LR

NY 182 704

Church of Scotland

Linked with St Andrew's Annan

4.8km (3 miles) north of Annan.

Three-bay Gothic church with pinnacled tower, built 1835 by Mrs Dirom of Mount Annan and friends. Interior recast 1900. Viscount two-manual electronic organ was gifted to the church in 2007. This beautiful little village church is at the highest point of the village and has a most peaceful sanctuary.

- Sunday: 10.00am
- Open by arrangement (01461 202626)

C

157 CLOSEBURN PARISH CHURCH

**Cample
Closeburn
DG3 5HD**

⚔ NX 904 923

🏠 Church of Scotland

Linked with Durisdeer

By Thornhill, off A76.

Built by James Barbour 1878 alongside former (1741) church. In Gothic style with a three-stage tower. Spacious interior with an elaborate hammerbeam roof supported on foliaged corbels. Pipe organ by Henry Willis & Sons 1887. Window in the north transept by the St Enoch Glass Studios 1948. Font originally from Dalgarnock. In the graveyard is the smart mausoleum built by Thomas Kirkpatrick of Closeburn in 1742.

- Sunday: 10.30am
- Open by arrangement (01848 500231)

158 DALTON KIRK

**Dalton
DG11 1DS**

⚔ NY 114 740

🏠 Church of Scotland

Linked with Hightae, Kettleholm

By Lockerbie on B725.

Close by the roofless shell of the 1704 parish church stands J. M. Dick Peddie's 1895 sturdy Romanesque church. Unusually colourful kingpost-truss roof over the nave and scissors roof in the chancel. Three-light stained glass window of the Ascension by A. Ballantine and Gardiner 1896. The graveyard contains a late Georgian burial enclosure and the suave classical monument to the Carruthers of Whitecroft.

- Sunday: 9.45am, 11.15am by rotation with Hightae and St Mungo Kettleholm
- Open by arrangement (01387 811499)

159 DORNOCK PARISH CHURCH

**Church Lane
Dornock
DG12 6SU**

 NY 230 660

Church of Scotland

Linked with Annan Old

6.4km (4 miles) east of Annan.

Traditional T-plan kirk of 1793 with round-headed windows and birdcage bellcote. Interior refurbished 1884 by James Barbour. Stained glass windows of *Christ the Good Shepherd* and *The Agony in the Garden* by Ballantine and Gardiner, 1893. Three richly carved ancient Hog Stones, probably 13th century, with Viking/Dane connection. There is no bell; it lies at the door of the sanctuary in Bowness-on-Solway on the English side, taken in reprisal for the theft by the Scots of the Bowness bell and its loss in the Solway.

- Sunday: 10.00am, in church, 2nd and 4th Sunday of month; in Baxter Hall 1st, 3rd and 5th
- Open by arrangement (01461 201405)

B

160 CRICHTON MEMORIAL CHURCH, DUMFRIES

**The Crichton
Bankend Road
Dumfries
DG1 4UQ**

 NX 983 742

Non-denominational

 www.crichton.co.uk

Cathedral-style church designed by architect Sydney Mitchell. Crichton Memorial Church completed in 1897. Square tower 37.5m (123ft) high. The richly detailed exterior is of red sandstone from Locharbriggs, Dumfries. The elegant interior features pink sandstone from nearby Thornhill. Ornate oak roof. Stone carving by William Vickers of Glasgow. The boldly designed floor is of Irish and Sicilian marble. Impressive stained glass by Oscar Paterson of Glasgow throughout. Pulpit and choir stalls date from 1897. The magnificent organ by Lewis 1902 has richly carved screens. Brass angel lectern 1910. Popular venue for weddings, concerts and other special events.

- Sunday: 9.00am; Thursday: 11.00am
- Open by arrangement with Crichton Development Company (01387 702020)

A WC

161 MAXWELLTOWN WEST CHURCH, DUMFRIES

**Laurieknowe
Dumfries
DG2 7AH**

⚔ NX 966 760

🏛 Church of Scotland

Built as Maxwelltown Free Church in 1866, the church was designed by James Barbour. An imposing church in red sandstone, it presents a Gothic façade to the street with two large windows over the central door, a pierced parapet to the gable and a central octagonal belfry. Galleries on three sides focus on the 20th-century pulpit in front of the organ, rebuilt in 1948. The war memorial gates were moved here from Laurieknowe Church in 1999.

- Sunday: 11.00am, except June to mid-August 10.00am
- Open by arrangement (01387 252929)

162 ST GEORGE'S, DUMFRIES

**50 George Street
Dumfries
DG1 1EJ**

⚔ NX 971 764

🏛 Church of Scotland

🌐 www.saint.georges.org.uk

Built as a Free Church in 1844 by William McGowan, and remodelled in 1893 by James Halliday who added the Italianate front of red sandstone. Almost square interior with north and south aisles marked off by superimposed Corinthian columns. Compartmented and coved main ceiling.

- Sunday: 11.00am; additionally July and August 9.30am (Family Service)
- Open by arrangement (01387 253696)

163 ST JOHN THE EVANGELIST, DUMFRIES

**Lovers Walk
Dumfries
DG1 1LW**

 NX 975 765

Scottish Episcopal

⊕ www.episcopaldumfries.org

Junction with Newall Terrace.

Red sandstone Gothic church designed by Slater & Carpenter and consecrated in 1868. Mosaic reredos by the Venice and Murano Glass and Mosaic Co., 1881. Engraved windows and glass doors in the porch by David Gulland, a member of the congregation, 2007, when a local ecumenical partnership (Scottish Episcopal / Methodist) was signed. Organ by Harrison & Harrison, 1938, refurbished 1969 and 2008.

- Sunday: 8.00am, 9.30am; on 1st and 2nd Sundays of the month, 11.00am and 6.00pm; Wednesday, 10.30am
- Open daily 9.00am–5.00pm

164 ST MICHAEL'S AND SOUTH PARISH CHURCH, DUMFRIES

**St Michael's Street
Dumfries
DG1 2QB**

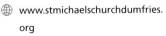 NX 975 757

Church of Scotland

⊕ www.stmichaelschurchdumfries. org

Written records go back to 1190 since when three churches have stood on the site. The pillars of the 1500 church were used in the present building (1741–6), raided by Bonnie Prince Charlie in 1745. Robert Burns worshipped here until his untimely death; his wife Jean Armour continued to worship for a further 38 years. This beautiful church has a fine collection of stained glass, some dating back to 1800. The Archangel St Michael overlooks the congregation from the front of the Willis organ. A wonderful church full of history and a warm welcome awaits visitors.

- Sunday: 11.00am
- Open Easter to September, Monday to Friday, 10.00am–4.00pm, or by arrangement (01387 255007)

165 DUNSCORE PARISH CHURCH

**Dunscore
DG2 0SZ**

NX 867 843

Church of Scotland

www.dunscorechurch.co.uk

Linked with Glencairn, St Ninian's Moniaive

On B729 in centre of village.

This handsome Gothic church, 1823–4 by James Thomson, sits in a prominent position in the village surrounded by its graveyard. The window surrounds and buttresses are painted white and contrast with the dark whinstone of the walls. The Square tower has a clock on three of its four faces. In excellent decorative and structural condition. Galleried interior. Electric organ and sound system record the services for the house-bound.

- Sunday: 10.00am or 11.45am; 7.00pm on 2nd Sunday of the month
- Open by arrangement (01387 820245 or 01387 820877) or keyholders' names at door of church

166 DURISDEER PARISH CHURCH

**Durisdeer
DG3 5BJ**

NS 894 038

Church of Scotland

Linked with Closeburn

1.6km (1 mile) east of A702.

Unspoilt, peaceful, Georgian country parish church, rebuilt 1716, topped by a belfry tower. X-plan, one arm of the cross is taller and more sophisticated, built for the Duke of Queensberry and remaining from the earlier church. Inside is the most amazing monument over the Queensberry burial vault, a baroque baldacchino carved in 1695 by John van Nost to the design of James Smith who was also architect of the later church. 'There are few buildings in which baroque magnificence and presbyterian decency are so happily combined' (George Hay, *Architecture of Scottish Post-Reformation Churches*). Martyr's Grave 1685. Drumlanrig Castle nearby.

- Sunday: 11.45am
- Open during daylight hours

 (Afternoon teas, Sundays, July, August and September)

167 ST JOHN THE EVANGELIST, EASTRIGGS

**Ladysmith Road
Eastriggs
DG12 6QE**

⚔ NY 248 663
⛪ Scottish Episcopal

Linked with St John's Annan, All Saints' Gretna, All Saints' Lockerbie, St John's Moffat

Junction with Dunedin Road.

Eastriggs built during the First World War to house munition workers; St John's was dedicated to serve the workers and was visited by King George V and Queen Mary. Designed in 1917 by C. M. Crickmer in association with Raymond Unwin, who designed the town. Charming and characterful church in early style with Arts & Crafts touches. Sturdy tower with pyramidal roof with swept eaves. Major repairs completed 2005 and church rededicated by the Primus of the Scottish Episcopal Church in 2008.

- Sunday: 11.00am
- Open by arrangement (01461 700171)

168 GLENCAIRN PARISH CHURCH

**Kirkland
DG3 4HD
NX 809 905**

⚔ Church of Scotland
⛪ www.glencairnparish.co.uk

Linked with St Ninian's Moniaive, Dunscore

On A702, 3.2km (2 miles) east of Moniaive.

Tall dignified T-plan Gothic style church given presence by a handsome square tower with tall pinnacles, 1836–7 by William McCandlish. Original box pews in the galleries, others of 1900 when improvements were carried out. Magnificent stained glass windows including *The Good Shepherd* by Abbey Studio. Bronze relief bust of Rev. Patrick Bannerman by James Paterson, 1900, on east gable. Pipework of organ (reported unserviceable in 1937) still in place. The graveyard contains the remains of the former church and several notable Covenanter gravestones.

- Sunday: 10.00am or 11.45am 4th Sunday of month
- Open by arrangement (01387 820245 or 01848 200307)

169 ALL SAINTS', GRETNA

**Annan Road
Gretna
DG16 5DH**

Ⓐ NY 318 673

 Scottish Episcopal

Linked with St John's Annan,
St John's Eastriggs, All Saints'
Lockerbie, St John's Moffat

Built in 1917 by the Ministry of
Munitions to serve the large Anglican
population working in the area's
armaments factories. Designed by
Geoffrey Lucas in early Christian
style, the nave roof sweeping out
over the aisles. The Arts & Crafts
furnishings: choir stalls, communion
rail, lectern and pulpit, were designed
by Lucas and the wood carving
executed by Lawrence Turner.
Substantial refurbishment has not
altered the fittings or the character. A
warm welcome awaits all who visit.

- Sunday: 10.45am
- Open by arrangement (01461 337533)

170 HIGHTAE KIRK

**Hightae
DG11 1JL**

Ⓐ NY 090 793

 Church of Scotland

Linked with Dalton, Kettleholm

On B7020, 4km (2½ miles) south of
Lochmaben.

Built as a Relief meeting house
in 1796 and remodelled for the
Reformed Presbyterians in 1865, when
the windows were enlarged and the
gabled west bellcote and small porch
were added.

- Sunday: 9.45am, 11.15am by
  rotation with Dalton and St Mungo
  Kettleholm
- Open by arrangement (01387 811499)

171 ST MUNGO PARISH CHURCH, KETTLEHOLM

**Kettleholm
DG11 1BU**

NY 143 771

Church of Scotland

Linked with Dalton, Hightae

On B723, 4.8km (3 miles) south of Lockerbie.

Built under the patronage of the Rt Hon. Robert Jardine MP of Castlemilk. Late Scots Gothic by David Bryce 1877 with a pinnacled-buttressed porch decorated with grotesque carved heads. Inside, a magnificently elaborate open roof. Organ 1905 by Abbot & Smith. Stained glass by James Ballantine & Son 1876. First World War memorial by F. M. Taubman.

- Sunday: 9.45am, 11.15am by rotation with Dalton and Hightae
- Open by arrangement (01387 811499)

172 KIRKMABRECK PARISH CHURCH

**Kirk Brae
Creetown
DG8 7DL**

NX 476 585

Church of Scotland

Off A75, 9.7km (6 miles) from Newton Stewart.

Imposing building with a square bell-tower above the front gable, built in 1834 by John Henderson. Panelling 1645 with Muir family coat of arms. In spring, churchyard and graveyard carpeted with crocuses.

- Sunday: 11.30am
- Open by arrangement (01671 820471)

173 KIRKMICHAEL KIRK

**Townhead
DG1 3LY**

Ⱶ NY 005 884
⌂ Church of Scotland
⊕ www.kirkinthor.co.uk

Linked with Tinwald, Torthorwald

Between Parkgate and Ae, off A701.

Built in 1815 in the location of churches thought to date from 9th and 10th centuries. Classic T-plan of rough dressed whinstone with sandstone facings, large round-headed windows and a birdcage bellcote. Three stained glass memorial windows (*Our Lord stilling the storm*, *Our Lord the Good Shepherd* and *Our Lady with Faith and Hope*), three memorial plaques and a laird's loft. Good collection of 18th-century stones in the graveyard.

• Sunday: 9.45am or 11.15am
• Open by arrangement (01687 860235 or 01387 86064

174 ST FRANCIS OF ASSISI, LANGHOLM

**Drove Road
Langholm
DG13 0JW**

Ⱶ NY 365 845
⌂ Roman Catholic

Linked with St Columba's Annan, Holy Trinity Lockerbie, St Luke's Moffat

Off High Street.

Built as a United Presbyterian Church, 1883–4 by Michael Brodie, now back in ecclesiastical use after a period of secularisation. A simple hall church of grey stone and with a slate roof topped with a flèche. Imposing porch with double doors and foliated capitals. Interior lit by stained glass lancet windows.

• Wednesday: 6.30pm
• Open by arrangement (01461 202776)

175 LOCHMABEN CHURCH

**High Street
Lochmaben
DG11 1NJ**

NY 083 823

Church of Scotland

Linked with Applegarth

South end of village on A709.

Rectangular Gothic church by James Thomson, 1820, with pinnacled tower. Original gated box pews in U-shaped gallery. Other pews and furnishings, 1880s. The Bruce Bell and Popes Bell are said to date back to the time of Robert the Bruce. Organ, 1903 by Walcker, renovated by Harrison & Harrison, 1994. Attractive wrought-iron organ screen portrays Christian symbols.

- Sunday: 11.30am
- Open by arrangement (01387 810486)

176 ALL SAINTS', LOCKERBIE

**Ashgrove Terrace
Lockerbie
DG11 2QB**

NY 134 818

Scottish Episcopal

Linked with St John's Annan, St John's Eastriggs, All Saints' Gretna, St John's Moffat

Picturesque Arts & Crafts church with tower and broach spire by John Douglas of Chester, consecrated 1903. Rich but delicate altarpiece by Sir Ninian Comper with Italian Renaissance-inspired blue and gold painted wooden panels above carved alabaster figures. Stained glass by Comper, Westlake and Morris & Co. Extension, added 2005, provides well-used meeting rooms.

- Sunday: 11.15am
- Open by arrangement (01576 202484)

177 HOLY TRINITY, LOCKERBIE

**Arthurs Place
Lockerbie
DG11 2DY**

Ⓐ NY 136 815

🏠 Roman Catholic

Linked with St Columba's Annan, St Francis Langholm, St Luke's Moffat

Built as Trinity Church 1874 for the United Presbyterian Church, became Church of Scotland 1929 and acquired in 1973 by the Catholic Church and renamed Holy Trinity. Designed by Ford Mackenzie, built in Corncockle sandstone in Gothic style with a large rose window and steeple. The organ, Ingram of Edinburgh, is a prominent feature. Plaque in vestibule commemorates 1,000 years of Christianity in Ukraine. Copy of Lockerbie Book of Remembrance and Memorial Plaque.

- Sunday: 10.30am
- Open daily 9.00am–4.00pm

178 ST ANDREW'S, MOFFAT

**Churchgate
Moffat
DG10 9EJ**

Ⓐ NT 785 051

🏠 Church of Scotland

🌐 www.standrewsmoffat.org.uk

Linked with Wamphray

Impressive church in Early English style by John Starforth 1884, with a central tower flanked by bowed stair towers. Richly carved entrance leads to a wide interior with galleries on slender iron columns. Profusion of stained glass including rose window above the pulpit by Starforth. Other windows by James Ballantine & Son, Ballantine & Gardiner, and William Meikle & Sons. Pipe organ by Eustace Ingram 1894.

- Sunday: 11.15am
- Open June to September, 10.30am–12.30pm and 2.00–4.00pm

179 ST JOHN THE EVANGELIST, MOFFAT

Burnside
Moffat
DG10 9DX

NT 087 053

Scottish Episcopal

Linked with St John's Annan, St John's Eastriggs, All Saints' Gretna, All Saints' Lockerbie

White-harled church of 1953, designed by Ian G. Lindsay in the style of a typical country church of the 18th century. It replaced a 'tin chapel' built of corrugated iron in 1872. Furnishings in appropriate Neo-Georgian style. Boer War memorial window of 1903 by C. E. Kempe from St Ninian's Preparatory School installed behind the altar in 1989. 'Father' Willis organ, recently restored.

- Sunday: 9.15am; Wednesday: 10.00am
- Open by arrangement (01683 221100)

180 ST LUKE'S, MOFFAT

Mansfield Place
Moffat
DG10 9DS

NT 086 053

Roman Catholic

Linked with St Columba's Annan, Holy Trinity Lockerbie, St Francis Langholm

Built in 1865 for the Episcopal community and used by them until their present church was built in 1872. Thereafter this building became the Mechanics' Hall until 1895 when it was reconsecrated for the Roman Catholic communion. Dark wood-clad walls and steep slated roof. Restored 1990.

- Sunday: 9.00am; Thursday: 10.00am
- Open by arrangement (01461 202776)

181 ST NINIAN'S PARISH CHURCH, MONIAIVE

**North Street
Moniaive
DG3 4HR**

Ⓐ NX 777 910

Church of Scotland

⊕ www.glencairnparish.co.uk

Linked with Glencairn, Dunscore

On A702.

Built 1887–8 as a chapel of ease, designed by W. West Neve. Tall narrow nave with side aisles. Simple Gothic windows adorn the gable and aisles. A continuous clerestory with stained glass and opening mechanism lights the nave. Major improvements were carried out 2006–8.

- Sunday: 10.00am or 11.45am 1st three Sundays of month
- Open by arrangement (01387 820245 or 01848 200307)

182 TINWALD CHURCH

**Tinwald
DG1 3PL**

Ⓐ NY 003 816

Church of Scotland

⊕ www.kirkinthor.co.uk

Linked with Kirkmichael, Torthorwald

Off A701, 4.8km (3 miles) north of Dumfries.

A plain rectangle with bell-finialled birdcage bellcote built in 1769 on the foundations of an earlier medieval church. Four stained glass windows by Gordon Webster. Interior, with fine hammerbeam roof, has the matching pews arranged to form a central aisle. Chancel area furnished in oak with octagonal pulpit, pedestal font, communion table and Minister's and Elders' chairs. Session Room added 2000. Covenanters' Monument in graveyard. Striking views over Nithsdale.

- Sunday: 9.45am or 11.15am
- Open by arrangement (01387 710551 or 01387 711196)

183 TORTHORWALD CHURCH

**Torthorwald
DG1 3QA**

⚔ NY 035 783

⛪ Church of Scotland

🌐 www.kirkinthor.co.uk

Linked with Kirkmichael, Tinwald

Off A709, 6.4km (4 miles) east of Dumfries.

A church was founded in Torthorwald in the mid-13th century by Trinitarian or Red Friars from Fail Monastery near Tarbolton, Ayrshire. A white T-plan kirk built in 1872 to replace an earlier church on an adjacent site, stones dated 1450 and 1644 are set into the walls of the vestry. Pipe organ 1904. The entrance gates are a memorial to Dr John G. Paton, a pioneer missionary to the islands of the South Pacific.

- Sunday: 9.45am or 11.25am
- Open by arrangement (01387 750245 or 01387 750673)

184 WAMPHRAY PARISH CHURCH

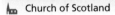

**Wamphray
DG10 9NF**

⚔ NY 107 948

⛪ Church of Scotland

Linked with St Andrew's Moffat

Across River Annan from Newton.

Neat rectangle by William McGowan 1834 with a slender bellcote. A carved medieval slab forms the lintel over the door. Notable 18th-century headstones in the graveyard and a monument to the Rt Rev. A. H. Charteris, Founder of The Woman's Guild and Moderator of the General Assembly in 1892.

- Sunday: 10.00am
- Open by arrangement (01576 470275)

185 **WESTERKIRK**

**Bentpath
DG13 0PG**

A NY 312 903

⌂ Church of Scotland/Scottish
Episcopal

On B709, 11.3km (7 miles) north-west of Langholm.

Pleasing Victorian church of 1881 by James Burnet, now fully restored from its former uninhabitable condition; restoration supervised by Richard Jaques of York. A fine organ of like period has been installed. Twelve new stained glass windows showing natural life in the Westerkirk valley, including a window commemorating the Golden Jubilee of 2002 donated by the community. In the graveyard is the Johnson Mausoleum, a classical Greek cross by Robert Adam 1790.

- Church of Scotland service 2.30pm on 1st Sunday (except July and August); Episcopal services approximately four times a year (see local press)
- Open by arrangement (01387 370201 / 381240 / 370215)

B (church) **A** (mausoleum)

Index

References are to each church's entry number in the gazetteer.